D0029541

© Steven Campbell/loco fx

About the Author

Kate Sciandra has been teaching in the realms of personal and spiritual development for over twenty years. She has been a professional integrative healthcare provider since 1993 and is registered with the State of Minnesota as a minister, having had an active meditation practice since 2001. Sciandra has a Diploma in Herbal Studies from the Australasian College of Herbal Studies, and is a Registered Instructor and Advanced Practitioner with the Society of Ortho-Bionomy International®.

THE
MINDFULNESS
HABIT

Six Weeks to Creating
the Habit of Being Present

KATE SCIANDRA

Llewellyn Publications
Woodbury, Minnesota

FIRST EDITION
First Printing, 2015

Book design by Bob Gaul
Cover art: www.iStockphoto.com/455341/©Zuki
Cover design by Lisa Novak
Hourglass graphic by Llewellyn Art Department

Llewellyn Publications is a registered trademark of Llewellyn Worldwide Ltd.

Library of Congress Cataloging-in-Publication Data
Sciandra, Kate, 1963–
  The mindfulness habit: six weeks to creating the habit of being
present/Kate Sciandra.—First Edition.
    pages cm
  Includes bibliographical references.
  ISBN 978-0-7387-4189-5
1. Meditation. 2. Meditation—Therapeutic use. I. Title.
BF637.M4S42 2015
158.1'2—dc23
                              2014033920

Llewellyn Worldwide Ltd. does not participate in, endorse, or have any authority or responsibility concerning private business transactions between our authors and the public.

All mail addressed to the author is forwarded, but the publisher cannot, unless specifically instructed by the author, give out an address or phone number.

Any Internet references contained in this work are current at publication time, but the publisher cannot guarantee that a specific location will continue to be maintained. Please refer to the publisher's website for links to authors' websites and other sources.

Llewellyn Publications, a Division of Llewellyn Worldwide Ltd.
2143 Wooddale Drive
Woodbury, MN 55125-2989
www.llewellyn.com
Printed in the United States of America

Contents

List of Exercises

Acknowledgments

Thanks to anyone who is family, by birth or by choice, for providing an invisible but reliable soft landing place that, whether or not I needed it, I always knew was there.

To all my teachers, in every place, of every stripe. Thanks to Mark Nunberg for your gentle encouragement, friendship, and hand-holding, to Richard Valasek for being my evil twin and modeling for me how to embrace my own role as an iconoclast, and to Tim Burkett for holding me carefully in his hands and heart as I struggled and as I blossomed.

Much gratitude for my *sangha*, and other providers of spiritual home and support for my personal development, especially GOM.

Special thanks to those who were generous enough to tell me their stories and to share their unique insights with me.

Lastly, special thanks to all of those people who have been my students over the years and, by extension, my teachers. Your questions, your enthusiasm, and your insights have made me better every single time. I value the trust you placed in me above all else.

Introduction

You've probably heard of mindfulness, and you may have heard that meditation would be a good way to improve your health and well-being, but inserting thirty minutes of meditation into your already over-full day seems impossible and, frankly, unappealing.

It is entirely possible to find a place for calming the body and quieting the mind in your schedule, no matter how busy it is. There are more opportunities for you to find a way to become present, centered, and mindful than you ever imagined, and you only need three things to take advantage of them: the ability to recognize them when they arise, the knowledge of what to do when they arise, and the intention and habit of doing it.

These three things are exactly what you'll get from discovering the gift of the present moment. What you'll get from those three things is a life that is illuminated by a sense of calm, focus, and contentment, that brings joy not only to you but to those whose lives you touch.

Welcome to your world of having a Mindfulness Habit.

I have been in places in my life where I have felt buried by my own distress, distraction, and worry, unable to understand that being without them was even possible. I have found myself up and awake in the middle of the night, my heart and mind racing, riddled with anxiety and worry. I have been so distracted that I had trouble finishing a sentence, let alone a thought. I have felt powerless. I have felt anger so intense that I have literally seen red. I have gone to dark, dark places in my mind and soul.

But now, I rarely get anywhere close to that angry—in fact, I don't get angry all that much. When I do, I recognize it, maybe even try to direct it constructively, and then I watch as it slips away. I sleep through the night without anxiety (most of the time), and my ability to be present and focused has taken me into an entirely different realm of functioning. I am more patient. I am more clear. I am more content and joyful.

Whether or not you are concerned about addressing these kinds of emotional and interpersonal issues, or just want to take better care of yourself, improve your concentration, and appreciate life more, you will benefit greatly from what you are about to learn.

You may have picked up this book because in some way you have reached a point where you feel you've had enough: enough tension, enough anxiety, enough stress-related health problems, and it is time for you to do something about it. You have decided that you are done with being depressed, anxious, unfocused, or angry. You are ready to move those feelings out of your life, change how you react to your problems and frustrations, and take the steps necessary to live in a place of joy and ease. You are reaching out for help. I'm going to throw you a rope and give you a tug in the direction of being able to have what I have found.

To some extent, we all struggle with anxiety, worry, and anger that we would like to live without. I am constantly amazed by the amount of discontent, suffering, stress, and low-grade anxiety that I see around me. The amount of suffering that good people carry can cause my heart to break. I feel sad, and yet I also feel optimistic.

I am sad because each and every one of us has everything we need to let some of that suffering slip away, feeling the weight lift off of our shoulders, including you. I can see it right there, but those who need it the most can't see it. And yet, it is this very fact that makes me optimistic as well, knowing that just below the surface there is a basic set of knowledge and understanding, tools that are right at hand that you can use to change your life for the better right now.

You may have found out that this need, this desire to move beyond tension, worry, drama, and anxiety often creates its own feelings of distress. Why? Because according to the books, TV shows, and magazine articles, there are lots of options for relieving stress.

They all make it sound so easy, but when you give them a closer look, these suggestions don't really seem to be something you can realistically picture yourself making a part of your life, a life filled with too much of some stuff and not nearly enough of the other stuff.

A yoga class? Not really you. A half hour of meditation? You barely find time to sleep. A vacation? That's not about to happen. An hour of "me" time? You're joking, right? There are so many suggestions for ways to help relieve yourself of the debilitating feelings of stress, but each brings its own set of problems, limitations, and hurdles with it. How will you find time? How can you learn to do this? How can you possibly find a way to fit it into your lifestyle? How can you afford it?

Trust me. Work with me. I've got your back.

Stop, sit back, and take a deep breath for a moment. In this book, I am going to meet you where you are, hold your hand, and give you bite-sized baby steps that you can follow, use, and integrate into your life—at work, with your kids, running errands, eating lunch, on your commute, or cleaning the house. These small, manageable steps are powerful, and they are possible.

Now give yourself a big thumbs-up, high-five, pat on the back, and an atta-girl/boy, because you have done something important. You are making a huge step. You have recognized that you do not have to live with this level of stress and discomfort. You have recognized that you can do something about it.

You are taking *action*.

Give yourself the gift of taking just a minute or two (okay, sometimes you'll need ten minutes) here and there over the next six weeks, and I promise, the world can open up to you. You will move into a place of patience, equanimity, kindness, focus, and luscious joy. This sounds like a big promise, but if you hold up your end, I will stick by it.

Are you game? Let's go.

How I Got Here

I began my own integrative healthcare practice in 1992. It was apparent to me that whatever I did with my time needed to serve others, and providing the opportunity for people to feel whole, well, and balanced was the best way for me to do so. I not only became a source for health and balance for other people, but I discovered that my real joy came from teaching others how to do the same. So besides my diploma in herbal studies and my advanced practitioner training in Ortho-Bionomy® (a kind of reeducation of the body and nervous system), I became a registered instructor.

One of my favorite things about teaching (and there are many things I love) is that it requires you to get really clear about what it is you are teaching. After all, you can't teach what you don't understand. The thing I wanted to get clear about was what I had learned over the years that made my work supportive and powerfully effective. I felt that if no other technique or individual fact stuck with my students, this way of approaching healing would.

Right about this time, I received an invitation to a Tibetan Medicine conference at the University of Minnesota. More often than not, when I get something like this I either recycle it immediately or I let it sit for a day or two, give it a couple of looks, and then into the bin it goes. But this mailer sat on my coffee table for days. Every day I would pick it up and look at it, and then put it back on the table. I could not stop thinking that I should be there. Finally, I gave up my resistance, surrendered to my instinct, and sent in my registration.

When at the conference, my feelings and thoughts about the deep connections between being a force for healing and being compassionate and present were reinforced. I felt like I was not only learning but being validated. I was particularly looking forward to the last day of the conference—the final benefit of enrollment was a ticket to attend a talk given by the Dalai Lama.

On a perfect May morning, I made my way over to Northrup Auditorium at the University of Minnesota. The grounds around the auditorium and the lobby were filled with Tibetan people dressed in their most fabulous clothing, the women striking in bright silks, the men dashing in their kilts.

Inside the auditorium itself, I was immersed in reading the extensive program when suddenly I had this very peculiar feeling.

It felt as though the building had tilted, or spun, or shifted dramatically in some way. Then I realized that everyone in the room was standing. The Dalai Lama had just walked onto the stage.

The talk he gave was in Tibetan, as it was designed to be a *dharma* talk (a talk about the teachings of the Buddha) for our large local Tibetan community. He would speak for quite a while, and then each long segment was translated into English by a charming—and obviously quite brilliant—fellow Tibetan. Sitting through long sections of a lecture that I was completely unable to understand should have been dull, but I was transfixed. By the time the Dalai Lama was halfway through his talk, I thought to myself, "I want whatever it is that *he* has." By the time I left, I had come to the realization that his gift was his ability to be completely present and utterly himself. And by "gift" I mean that this was not only his talent, but literally a gift he gave the world.

I needed to think some more about what that meant and how he was able to do this. I started reading and researching.

From that point on, I became fascinated by and dedicated to the understanding of being completely mindful and present. I found a teacher, and I started to practice mindfulness and meditation. My teacher helped me see the instinctive connection I was making between my work and mindfulness practice. When I saw this connection, I knew that it was the thing I'd been looking for to really fill out my Ortho-Bionomy classes.

How that manifested for me is another story, but I will say that learning to be present began to suffuse my life, my relationships, and, profoundly, my work. The more I saw the way it changed my work for the better, and the more I realized how much potential for a healthier mind and body it held, the more I started sharing it with clients and students, and the more I saw it change lives, especially my own.

Soon I began teaching what I'd learned about being present. I taught at yoga studios, at cafés, with sports teams, and at fitness centers. People loved the way things changed for them, even after one week. I wanted more and more of them to be exposed to their potential for this kind of well-being.

Since I began this journey, the amount of calm, compassion, and focus I am capable of has expanded, and continues to expand since I began to allow myself to understand what it means to be present. That expansion now needs to move beyond me, even beyond my clients, to anyone and everyone I can reach.

My goal for what I want you to get out of this book is to help you create three things. First, I want you to be able to recognize the places in your life that provide you the opportunity to create a focused, quiet mind. Next, I want you to know what you can do to take advantage of those moments of possibility when they present themselves. And third, I want you to notice how your ability to handle or respond to stressful situations, as well as your tendency toward worry, anxiety, and distraction, diminishes over time as you form the habits of mindfulness and integrate them into your lifestyle.

What I want most of all is a world full of people who are happy, resilient, and authentic, because that is the world I want to live in. Not only will I then share the planet with people like you who have learned how to live in the present with calm and clarity, but the positive ripples you will create as you intersect and interact with others has possibilities for changing the world beyond what we can even begin to imagine.

Take a minute and imagine how it would feel if you were surrounded by people who modeled the kind of calm presence that you would like to embody yourself. How would it be? Pleasant? Lovely? Easy? Think of how it would affect the way you go about things and how you would respond to other people. It's a kind of passive pay-it-forward. When you are patient and calm, you offset the anxiety of others, dispersing its energy. By embodying the easy-going, total, and authentic presence that you are capable of, you set off ripples that move out, further and further, far beyond where you can see.

When my daughter was tiny and threw the occasional tantrum, her dad and I could not help but begin to find it funny after a while. Our laughter dissolved those tantrums almost instantly. It's hard to be angry when people are laughing. It's hard to keep your anxiety up in the face of calm. Feed it no energy, and it loses steam like a hurricane hitting cold water.

You have taken the first step to being one of those people who creates that sense of calm. So you are not only creating a better life for yourself but for other people, some of whom you'll never meet. In the long run, it all comes back to creating a better place for you too. The cleaner the pond, the happier *all* the fish are.

Working with a Friend or Group

You may want to consider going through this program with a friend, or maybe your book club, or a group from your neighborhood, school, or spiritual community, setting up a time to meet on a regular basis to check in and share your progress, frustrations, and experiences.

This idea has many advantages for helping you find greater success. First of all, if you are at all like me, one of the absolutely best ways to make a firm commitment to a new undertaking is to make a commitment to someone else. If you have made that promise to show up for another person—or several others—it is far more likely you will keep up with the program and be more likely to complete it.

Another important thing that you can gain by working with others is support, someone else to bounce ideas, experiences, and questions off of. This has the advantage of providing the power of collaboration, a "two heads are better than one" environment when it comes to solving problems and making discoveries. It can be very heartening to know that the stumbling blocks you encounter are probably not yours alone, that others have similar struggles and doubts, so you feel less alone and gain more confidence.

Having a community, a *sangha*, provides a platform of support for your efforts, encouragement when you need it, and gentle warnings when you are moving in a direction that might be problematic or misguided.

Lastly, it is nice to have someone with whom you can celebrate your victories, large or small, as you gain new skills, open up your ability to be more present, and discover the benefits as they reveal themselves.

How This Book Works

This book contains techniques and exercises, but it's much more than that. It provides the foundation that you need to create a new way of living your life. The materials included in this book, if used with regularity and commitment, will help you create the habit of being more present and mindful in your life in a way that is seamless and integrated.

In each chapter you will find the following:

+ Information about a variety of topics related to being present, the benefits of mindfulness, habit formation, meditation, and other important basics

+ Instructions for exercises and techniques for exploring mindfulness

◆ Questions to deepen your understanding of
the material, to support you in fully integrating
the lessons, and to make the information your own

◆ Practices that are specifically designed to build
your habit of seeing your opportunities to be
in the present moment

One thing you will need before you begin is a journal. The most important thing in choosing your journal is that it be useful to you. You can buy a small pocket notebook, a pretty blank book, or a plain old spiral notebook at the local drugstore. If you already keep a journal, you can certainly use that as well. Are you someone who keeps your life on your tablet, phone, or other electronic device? If so, then set up a file there, if that's more appealing. Take the time to consider the method you are most likely to find easy to use, because that is the one that will work for you. Keep in mind that you may want to carry your journal with you to work, school, or other outings.

You'll be using your journal for a couple of different things. One is to keep track of your activities over the next several weeks as a way of helping you develop your new habit of being more present and mindful, and the other is to have a place to record your answers to the questions that follow the lessons and exercises. This allows you to keep everything in one place, creating a nice record of your journey that is fun and useful to review as you go through the process of creating your habit.

You'll learn more about how to use your journal as we go through the lessons and habit-building exercises, but you'll want to decide the basics of what format will work best for you so you can be ready to get started.

Now to learn more about how this book is supposed to work. It is designed to help you understand the value of living in the moment and what you can gain from the experience. It will teach you about the simple things you can do to bring you into living in the moment and the ways that you can fit those things easily into your work and home life. Finally, it will support you as you create the habit of finding opportunities to practice mindfulness.

Everyone learns differently. Some people experience things physically, while others enter the world through listening or seeing. Most of us are some combination of these. That is one reason why the information in this course is set up the way it is. It approaches each week using written material, visualizations, and body-centered lessons. This does three things: It reaches you, no matter what your predominant learning style is. It uses multiple ways of disseminating information, making it more likely you will understand, retain, and recall it when you need it. It gives you choices and options to draw from that fit what you're doing and how you are feeling in a variety of moods and situations.

The material in the book is divided up to be worked with over a period of six weeks. The time frame was specifically designed this way for a few reasons. First, spreading things out will keep you from feeling stressed about the amount of time you need to dedicate to the book and each lesson. Keeping the information "bite-sized" prevents you from trying to integrate too much at one time and feeling frustrated or overwhelmed.

Also, I want the new things you are learning to be easy to integrate into your life each week. Adding just a very few things at a time allows you to give each of them your attention and not feel like you are trying to juggle a lot of stuff at once.

Lastly, and crucially, taking this time creates a structure that will support habit development, so that by the end you will be seeing the opportunities to be present everywhere without having to try very hard; they'll begin to just arise in your awareness.

After you finish this introductory material, you will begin Week 1. Read the lesson and answer the questions in it. Then read through the exercises at least once, or better, twice, before practicing them. Then answer the questions about your experience. These questions will enable you to look more deeply at your experience, understand it better, and root it more deeply. Don't skip them.

Each week's reading ends with instructions for what you will want to practice over the next week (or five to nine days—I understand that sometimes flexibility is important; it's better to complete the task than to rush it, but do try not to fall too far behind). Do whatever you have to in order to get yourself to practice, use your journal, and give yourself the ten minutes per day or so that you need to use what you've learned.

Another thing that will help you is to understand my two rules. Rules? Well, really one rule and one strong suggestion.

The rule is: Be your own best friend. What does that mean? I mean that I want you to be sure to practice two important things. I want you to be gentle and supportive with yourself, and I want you to give yourself permission to be a beginner.

This means that you need to be patient, forgiving, and kind to yourself. If at any time you find yourself beginning to feel frustrated, impatient, or even angry with yourself, then it is time to stop. Just for a moment, stop and remember to be kind to yourself. You are not going to be perfect at anything right off the bat. If you need to, go get yourself a cup of tea, put your feet up, go for a walk around the block, or do a few stretches. Then come back and congratulate yourself for being here, for showing up, for making the effort in the first place. Think about this: would you scold someone else the way you're scolding yourself?

It's likely that you find that you may be not very good at everything you are learning, and that even though something may look simple, simplicity is always more complicated than it appears. Also remind yourself that all techniques are easier for some people than for others and that if you had mastered it, you'd already be doing it, and wouldn't have come here looking for help. All that is asked of you is to give the technique careful attention and genuine effort. If you bring those two things, it will come to you. And if it doesn't, that technique is just not for you right now. You can come back to it when you're in a different place in your availability, understanding, or patience, and maybe it will work for you then.

Everyone will have techniques that work best for them: best for their lifestyle, for their learning style, for their way of interacting with the world. This is why I will be giving you a lot of options, so that you can choose what works for you, no matter your circumstances, style, and mood.

As for the strong suggestion? Do the work. All the work. Use the support materials, even if they seem extra, unnecessary, or goofy. Practice every day. There's really not a big time commitment in doing it, and to get the most out of your investment, use everything at your disposal. Jump in with both feet. Invest the time and attention and make the next twenty, forty, or sixty years healthier, happier, and more wonderful.

In fact, I am sure that after a short while of making this kind of everyday mindfulness part of your life, you will suddenly one day find yourself surprised and appreciative of the huge difference it has made in how you look at the world, feel about your experiences, and relate to other people.

Don't worry: the work and time required are not overwhelming, and most of the exercises are things that fit into what you are already doing (that's the point, right?). *If you really want to cultivate the habit of integrating and using the things you will be learning, the exercises are very important.* Make them a regular part of your day, and the changes will be profound. In my experience, most people notice some very cool things happening before the six weeks are over.

Now I want you to put your hand over your heart, and pledge that you will give yourself this great and beautiful gift, that you will not skimp on the time you dedicate to this process, and that you accept that it is an easy, ten-minute mini-break in your day that will reap huge rewards.

Get rid of "I should," tune your mind into "I get to …" and let's have a blast.

CHAPTER 1

Week 1

Peace Lives in the Present

"If you are depressed, you are living in the past. If you are anxious, you are living in the future. If you are content, you are living in the present." Maybe you've seen this quote, or something like it, and said to yourself, "Yes! I am tired of being depressed. I am tired of being worried. I no longer want to be anxious. I am going to live in the present!" And although you mean it, and mean it with all your heart, that's as far as it gets, because despite your best intentions, you don't really have a plan for exactly *how* you would go about it.

Besides coming to the realization that you're not sure of what to do, you also find that *remembering* to practice what you *do* know simply becomes one more thing for you to put on your to-do list, one more thing to think and worry about.

That is why I am going to provide a place where you will learn some basic skills for living in the present, outside of the depression-creating past and the anxiety-producing future. Learning how to be entirely here, right now, is a chance to experience your life more fully, seeing the beauty of the moment, even when things are difficult. It is an opportunity for quieting and soothing yourself, creating a more spacious mind, and a more relaxed body.

The present is the place where we can experience the power of being alive most fully, and yet we cheat ourselves out of the gift of being there over and over again.

These are some of the things that I've learned can happen when you are living in the present:

Anger has little energy. It's not that you will not experience anger; it just doesn't have the charge, or the stamina to last, that it used to.

Carrying a grudge is difficult. Grudges require regular trips through time into the past. Once you get used to being in the present, you find they are something you can easily live without.

Worrying is not possible. This is not to say that you won't find yourself occasionally slipping into worry; it's that you won't do it as frequently, and when you do, you can recognize it and "rescue" yourself easily by simply bringing your attention back to the present moment.

Time slows down. This sounds crazy at first, but when you are completely in the present moment, that moment is so rich and so full of life, and you can see events unfold so clearly. The result is that you see the millions of little moments inside each big one.

The creative mind is set free. Clearing out the worry, anxiety, list making, and busy chatter creates space for your mind to run and be inspired, when you are ready for that to happen.

Physical pain diminishes and sometimes disappears. This is another one that seems unlikely, but it's true. For example, studies have shown that worry contributes significantly to increased perception of pain. This is just one of the ways that being present has a positive effect on your experience of pain.

The everyday becomes richer and more enjoyable. Seriously. Tastes are more exciting, sounds are richer, and colors are brighter when your attention is allowed to rest solely on your immediate experience.

Slipping into the present moment is a gift you give to yourself and to others. Your increased patience and kindness, and your increasingly more balanced approach to life, become a balm to others around you and make you feel great.

The only thing you need to learn in order to live in the present is how to be mindful. Simple. But it takes practice.

Where Does All the Stress Come From?

The thing we call "stress" is an individual experience. It's a word that wasn't even defined in the way we use it now until well into the twentieth century. Before that, it was a term used in physics to describe a property of elasticity.

In the 1930s, a researcher named Hans Selye rechristened the word to mean a body's response to a demand for change. He experimented with subjecting laboratory animals to everything from temperature extremes and loud noise to perpetual frustration.

What happened? The animals exhibited resulting physical symptoms such as heart attack, stroke, kidney failure, and rheumatoid arthritis. These body symptoms correlate with the problems that humans have when they find themselves frustrated and subject to perpetual discomfort.

The things that produce a sense of anxiety or being overwhelmed in one person can have no effect—or even a positive effect—on another. A good example of this is the way introverts and extroverts interact with the world, how they find peace and replenishment, and what aspects of social interaction they find most difficult.

We create our own stress when we practice what I call "time travel." As I mentioned at the beginning of the chapter, we leave the present moment anytime we get caught up in the events of the past or anticipate those of the future. Planning is good; worrying, fretting, and anticipating are not good. Even anticipating something good sets you up for rejecting the gift of being here and now, and worst of all, all too often it sets you up for disappointment.

I'll tell you more about how to plan and remember without obsessing, worrying, or stewing later in the book, but for now, it's just good to know that these are ways of thinking that can create a lot of distress and discomfort for your already tired mind.

And speaking of tired minds, not taking the opportunities that are around you to coax your mind into becoming quiet and peaceful does nothing to help that tired mind from becoming exhausted, and yet most people don't bother to do so. I believe this is because they have no context for understanding what it means to have a quiet mind. Because most people have never taken the time to stop and pay attention to what their mind is doing, they may have never had a quiet mind. Or they may not have known what it was when they stumbled luckily into the blissful sense of being present, and therefore don't recognize it for what it is and don't know how to re-create it. They only know that for that moment, they felt alive, calm, and peaceful.

Why is it so hard for your mind to be peaceful and quiet? If you think about it, you may realize that you are constantly subjected to sensory input that your mind is always actively processing, even when you may not realize it is—daydreaming is thinking, too!

You read: reports for work, books, magazines, blogs, and websites.

You talk: conversations with friends, coworkers, and the guy who makes your coffee.

You think: solve problems; remember lists, numbers, or errands; and keep track of your toddler, your schedule, and maybe everyone else's schedule too.

Even when you don't believe you're thinking, you are. You have a mental commentary running, and often you are completely unaware of how much of it is going on. For two or three seconds, close your eyes, and do nothing. What do you notice? It only takes a moment to hear the jabbering, the running commentary that permeates our thoughts almost all the time.

This busy, hectic mind contributes significantly to creating the state we've come to refer to as stress.

Not only is the hyperactive brain tiring, but that busy mind often keeps you awake at night, and sleeplessness makes everything difficult as you function less efficiently and less effectively while being short-tempered and physically uncomfortable.

Let's face it, life can be hard. Evolution prepared us to live in a world where our causes for worry and panic were about whether we could find enough fruit or roots to keep us alive, and whether we could outrun that tiger. Now we worry about our relationships, our jobs, and whether Social Security will still be there for us when we need it. We worry about social unrest, global warming, terrorist attacks, the banking system, and how we'll pay for college. How much longer will the roof last? How about the car? Am I dressed appropriately for Casual Friday? It starts to make roots, fruits, and tigers look pretty straightforward, doesn't it?

The fight-or-flight response to difficult situations has a distinct set of physiological actions, from increased heart rate to changes in peripheral vision. These reactions are good in that they are designed to keep us alive if we need to run from or fight off an attacker, but have very limited practical application in the modern world. In fact, they can actually be more problematic than useful.

This constant state of low-grade stress is not what our bodies are built to handle, and it wears us down. It makes you feel out of control, it distracts you with worry, and it keeps you from enjoying the people, places, and things that are here, in front of you, every second of every day.

Stress makes everything that's already hard even harder. It makes you feel distracted rather than allowing you to be focused. It makes you more likely to react without thinking, rather than responding with clarity and patience. It makes you harder to be around rather than being fun to spend time with. It makes you run around more and get less done, rather than having a sense of calm purpose.

As I mentioned, stress is a significant contributor to health problems. The responses that our bodies evolved with over time to handle short, immediate events of danger are doing us harm in our modern world of constant, low-grade stressors. The physiological response that can save your life could also be slowly killing you. Your blood pressure and blood vessel health, heart, adrenal glands, and digestion (just for starters) show effects of consistent and regular exposure to feelings of tension and anxiety in ways that are definitely very unhealthy.

Besides the heart and blood vessel trouble that produce heart attacks and increase the likelihood of stroke that Hans Selye discovered, more recent discoveries about the effects of stress show that it has repercussions far beyond what you may have ever suspected. The increased levels of cortisol that are part of the fight-or-flight response to stressful situations can cause problems from weight gain to increased colds. Stress has been found to have an adverse effect on cancer treatment, as well as increasing the odds of having chronic health problems. One of these long-term chronic problems can be the result of the actual shrinking of the brain in response to repeated stress.

I am not sharing this to make you feel even *more* anxious. I am hoping that this will help you understand that this is important, and that your commitment to doing something about this can make a positive impact on more than just your attitude.

This is something so simple that you can do so easily, and it could save your life.

So you know that going through life feeling tense, pressured, and distracted is not good for you, and it's not fun. There are a lot of suggestions for ways to relieve this kind of pressure, but they seem to involve scheduling more stuff into your already overburdened lifestyle. And even if you do start going to yoga class twice a week, what do you do in between, when stuff comes up that makes everything feel like it's all just too much?

What I've learned, after many years of struggling myself, is that for every situation that pushes your buttons, prods you into worry, spins you out, or brings you down, there are even more opportunities to do the things that will help you develop a mind that is flexible, open, peaceful, calm, and responsive. When you learn how to spot and to take advantage of these opportunities, you begin to live with more joy and more ease.

Learning to be present is the antidote to the body's responses to stress. Stress, worry, and anxiety lose their power when they are observed with a quiet mind. It's like a superpower, but it is one you have to practice in order to make the best use of it. Mindfulness allows your thoughts and feelings to arise and then to pass without you clinging to them or feeling the need to push them away.

A mind that can be relaxed and present is like a body that is both strong and flexible. A flexible body can respond easily and quickly to sudden changes and adverse conditions. It adapts without causing additional stress to the structures of the body. A quiet, mindful presence creates a mind that is like that—a mind that can notice change and adversity and be effortlessly responsive without causing further distress.

The clarity that comes from a quiet mind gives room to observe and put in context your experiences and your responses to them. Noticing that you're sweating, your heart is racing, or your muscles have moved into a more tense, reactive state helps you realize your relationship to the object of your concern more objectively. Shining a little light on the situation is often all that is needed to make it disappear. A little attention is often all we need, and cultivating a state of mindfulness gives you the opportunity to provide that.

Understanding Mindfulness and Meditation

There has been so much buzz and talk about meditation and mindfulness. It's everywhere; everyone says it's good for your body, helps you feel less stressed, and makes living easier, but why? How does it do that?

In my experience, meditation is a valuable tool, but a formal meditation practice is not necessarily the right thing for everyone at every time in their life. It might be because of time, or because of interest, but bringing the *principles* of mindfulness meditation to the life you are already living is always appropriate, and profoundly helpful for everyone and anyone.

You may have heard of mindfulness in context with meditation, and this may have caused you some confusion. Your confusion is understandable; they are very much related to each other, and the names are sometimes used interchangeably, but they are different, and that difference is easy to understand.

I like to define mindfulness most simply and straightforwardly as coming to your senses by paying attention. This means it is something that can be done without any special equipment or dedication of time or other resources, only attention.

Meditation, although it sometimes involves the use of mindfulness, is different. Meditation is a blanket term for a variety of techniques. The thing they have in common is they produce a state in which your body is consciously relaxed and the mind is allowed to become calm and focused.

Some of the activities that are called meditation include the use of movement, chanting, or repeating mantras. Some of them have the meditator visualize images or employ prayer. Some of these employ mindfulness as part of them; some do not.

Meditation is one way to practice mindfulness, but it is not the only way. As a regular meditator, I find meditation to be a profoundly wonderful thing, but I don't want you to worry about that now. At this time, we're just working toward staying in the present moment. And *that* is a wonderful thing.

Everyone comes into learning something new with a set of assumptions. It's only natural that you may have some preconceived ideas, beliefs, and impressions about the words "meditation" and "mindfulness."

I'm a big believer in shining a light on anything that comes into the room so we can take a good look at it. This keeps things from sneaking in unawares and spoiling the fun for everyone. Your assumptions can be positive, negative, or a combination. Recognizing that you have them and what they are will take you a long way toward releasing any prejudices that might get between you and your ability to learn, accept, and absorb, as well as keeping you from disappointment. If we take the time to do this, it will allow you to begin this journey with your mind fresh and open to receiving this information, getting the most out of it.

So let's begin by bringing awareness to any of your assumptions, preconceptions, and misunderstandings. This is the first step in letting them go.

Here is your first exercise. You will want to get your journal out.

⏳ Exercise 1-1: Recognizing Your Preconceptions

Take a deep, relaxed breath or two, and settle into your body. Pay attention not only to what you think but how you feel in your body when you consider the following, and answer the questions in your journal.

Think of the word *meditation*. Say it quietly to yourself. Notice the first things that come to mind.

+ What do you think of when you hear the word *meditation*?

+ How did you *feel* when you answered the question above? What did you notice? Describe it as thoroughly as you can.

Think of the word *mindful*. Say it quietly to yourself. Notice the first things that come to mind.

+ What do you think of when you hear the word *mindful*?

+ How did you *feel* when you answered the question above? What did you notice? Describe it as thoroughly as you can.

Now look at how you responded to the two words. Is there a difference in how you feel about them, or do you feel the same way about them? Does talking about either or both of these words bring up any feelings of resistance? Which of these words describe your feelings or beliefs about *meditation*?

+ Time-consuming

+ Ineffective, pointless

+ Unpleasant, dull, "fun sucking"

- Nihilistic, ascetic, boring, abstemious

- Overly disciplined, rigid

- Complicated, difficult

- New Age, woo-woo, flakey

- Overly religious, incompatible with my
  religious beliefs

- Other:

Which of these words describe your feelings or beliefs about
mindfulness?

- Distracting

- Meaningless buzzword

- Unpleasant, dull, "fun sucking"

- Hyper-disciplined, rigid

- Redundant, not sure how this is different from what
  I'm already doing

- Complicated, difficult

- New Age, woo-woo, flakey

- Overly religious, incompatible with my
  religious beliefs

- Other:

Did you notice the number of assumptions and beliefs you have about entering into this process? Did it surprise you?

If you don't address and acknowledge these beliefs right away, any resistance you might have is going to keep you from entering into the process fully, and you won't be able to get the most out if it that you possibly can. Or if you have any romanticized notions about what you might be about to experience, you could find yourself disappointed. Fresh eyes and an open heart are the best things you can bring to the table.

We won't address all of these concerns right away. I am going to ask you to trust me and to know that over the process of this book, you will see many of your assumptions gradually addressed, and you will watch them fall away. But we're not going to get very far if we don't look at some of the big ones, so let's get a couple of them out of the way.

Developing a Common Vocabulary

First of all, let's agree on some basic definitions. As we saw before, there are many different activities that are described as meditation, so let's look at the definition that I am going to be using for our purposes. What we will call **meditation** is a set of techniques for quieting the mind by focusing your attention on a simple, defined subject. Despite what you may have heard, meditation is not something you do to *empty* your mind, but to *quiet* your mind.

Frankly, the idea of emptying my mind makes me feel kind of uncomfortable.

Mindfulness, on the other hand, is the skill of being able to be completely present with your actions, your environment, or your companions. Mindfulness is a skill that is necessary when meditating, but it is useful at all other sorts of times as well. By practicing mindfulness in any and every activity, you begin to bring some of the benefits of meditation into your life without having to set aside a separate time to practice it.

Now let's address the last belief on the list, the one concerned with **religion**. I want to assure you right up front that although many people see meditation as an integral part of their spiritual practice, it is not an inherently religious practice. Besides Buddhists, I have known Lutherans, Jews, Catholics, and Wiccans who use this information to quiet their mind and relieve their stress, worry, and anxiety. I've also known agnostics, atheists, and people with a vaguely spiritual bent who enjoy, and find useful, using mindfulness in their daily lives.

I sometimes describe these techniques for quieting the mind as mental hygiene. What you'll be learning has more in common with brushing your teeth than going to church, temple, or sacred grove. Some religious traditions do use a particular style of quiet contemplation that they refer to as meditation, but I believe that there is no component of the material in this book that will fly in the face of your existing religious beliefs nor inflict any upon you.

What you are learning here will make you a better person. It will allow you to be more focused, calm, patient, and kind. It will improve your ability to cope when the inevitable truck full of manure gets dropped in your path. If you consider that spiritual, and it helps you to do so, then I will not discourage you from embracing it on that level.

It is not worship; it is living, and living with fullness and clarity. I don't think you can object to that whether you are an Orthodox Jew, an atheist, a Quaker, or a conservative Catholic.

There is a bonus for you if you are someone with a strong relationship to your religious tradition. Some people find that a quieter mind gives them an opportunity to be more open to their connection with the divine, that the quiet mind is fertile ground for experiencing a union with the divine spirit they are in relationship with.

As for the idea that this material is flakey or weird, I will tell you that the modern scientific community has spent a great deal of time researching the benefits of quieting the mind. The Mayo Clinic recognizes it as a good health practice, as do many large corporations that make this information available to their employees. This is pretty straightforward stuff. If I mention anything esoteric, it will be more of a sidebar, a metaphor, or an illustration than something that you need to completely embrace in order to get the most out of what you are learning.

To address another concern or preconception, if you are concerned about needing to carve out a lot of time to do this, it is likely that one of the reasons you chose my approach over some other is because I promised you, up front, that this was about bringing that quiet mind and sense of being in the present into your life in ways that fit naturally and easily into your lifestyle. You will see that meditative awareness, or mindful living, fits over your life like a custom-made glove. It will even gradually, gently help shape the life you know now into one that you like a little better.

I have found that, in fact, mindfulness can help you discover *more* time in your schedule. (I know that sounds a little odd or counterintuitive, but we'll talk more about that later.)

As I said, you will discover the truth about some of the other things on the list as we go along. So get a drink of water, find a comfortable seat, and settle in.

The Air You Breathe

You breathe all the time—when you are asleep, awake, resting, exercising. You sometimes breathe quickly or slowly, shallow or deep, but stopping breathing by holding your breath takes a lot of effort. Breathing is an activity of the most fundamental, basic, nonthinking part of your brain, along with heartbeat, digestion, and so on.

Breathing is living, and not breathing—well, that would be a big problem. How you are breathing right now is more than just an exchange of oxygen and carbon dioxide. It is an expression of where your body and mind are at the moment. It is also a reflection of where they may have been in the past.

Lots of things affect your breathing, and when your breathing is not as relaxed or expansive as it should be, it causes you to feel more anxious. Learning about how your breathing affects the way you feel can also help you learn that changing your breath can help you feel more relaxed, open, and present.

Lots of different things can cause your breathing to be restricted. The first is a common one; it comes from what we've been hearing for a long time about what is correct and incorrect. We've been told that letting our bellies be relaxed and expansive when we breathe is a bad thing. The military-style posture that generations were taught as being ideal actually restricts your ability to breathe properly.

Sometimes clothing, such as ill-fitting bras or too-tight waistbands, can restrict breathing in a subtle but powerful way. This limitation is something you may not be aware of, but the more you get in touch with your breathing and tune in to what makes it harder and easier, the more you become aware of it.

Experiencing a physical or emotional trauma can cause the muscles that participate in breathing to "freeze" or become stuck, keeping you from breathing to your full capacity. Your body develops a habit of holding your breath, as if you are "waiting for the other shoe to drop," so that you don't exhale completely or inhale deeply. This is a common pattern if you unconsciously want to become less visible.

Of course, there are physiological reasons for restricted breathing as well. Disease or illness can make a difference in breathing, and smoking can have a profound effect on it too.

Your breathing changes with exertion, environment, emotional state, and level of concentration, among other things, and most of us are not using our breathing to its best advantage. The result is that you are not only changing the way you feel physically but the way you feel emotionally.

One of the most important causes of a change in how your body experiences breathing is your emotional state. Think back on the last time you cried really hard, and remember that kind of ragged, sobbing breath. Compare that to the kind of deep breathing you might do when you are in the middle of a good, fast walk, or to the shallow, breathless feeling you get when talking to your latest crush.

Take a moment now and choose a feeling. Think of what it is like to be fearful, angry, or gleeful. Now notice what that feels like in your body and breath.

Certainly how we feel strongly determines how we breathe. I often tell my clients that a big reason people don't breathe fully and deeply is because if they don't, they don't have to feel some of their feelings—usually uncomfortable ones. When you want to withhold experiencing your emotions, you hold your breath.

This is a very effective way to keep from having to look at those feelings you'd like to avoid. By the way, this is neither a very healthy nor effective strategy in the long term. Things like that have a way of coming out sideways.

The next exercise is going to play with an exploration of breathing and feelings. Get your journal ready. You'll be needing to answer some questions, so open to a fresh page and have something to write with handy as we begin.

Exercise 1-2: Your Breathing Affects Your Feelings

The habit of holding your breathing muscles in a suspended state of tension actually creates tension of another kind. Try this experiment:

Get yourself into a comfortable, upright, seated position. Close your eyes and just notice how you feel. Don't worry about being too detailed, but ask yourself the following questions.

In this very moment, answer quickly, on a scale of one to ten:

+ How optimistic do you feel?

+ How happy are you?

+ How afraid are you?

+ How much energy do you have?

+ How quiet or calm is your mind?

+ How relaxed is your body?

Sit quietly for a moment, following your breath, and then at some point in your breathing cycle, suddenly freeze the muscles in your rib cage. Now continue to breathe while keeping those muscles frozen and held in a state of tension.

As you continue to breathe in this restricted fashion, notice how you feel.

Again, on a scale of one to ten:

+ How optimistic do you feel?

+ How happy are you?

+ How afraid are you?

+ How much energy do you have?

+ How quiet or calm is your mind?

+ How relaxed is your body?

Are you feeling frightened, sad, or anxious? Do you find tension creeping into other parts of your body, like your shoulders, neck, or face—or maybe somewhere else? What is your mind like? Are your thoughts calm, or is your mind racing?

Are you beginning to see the relationship between your body's state and your emotional state? Calming the body can calm the mind; calming the mind has a similar effect on the body. It reverses the snowballing that happens when our reactive mind creates physical tension and that tension reminds us that we should be worried.

Now it is time to learn some things you can practice as part of developing a more present, quiet mind. The following exercises are beautiful ways to begin your journey. They pack a lot of punch into a little bit of effort. They are ways of using your breath that slow down and open up your breathing, a great thing to start with when you are feeling worried or overwhelmed as they have an immediate physical effect that shifts your agitated mind state right away.

But that's not all they do. They also provide a distinct point of focus for your mind. They are just complex enough to engage your attention, but simple enough that they won't get your brain thinking them through on a big, noisy track. When you are starting out, it's good to have something that will be just enough to engage your attention, something with built-in concentration.

A really great thing about using your breath as a tool is that you always have it with you, all the time. You can use it anywhere, relatively unobtrusively. It requires no special equipment, shoes, chair, or room. You don't need any space at all, other than what is required for your actual physical body. Working with breathing will be a great support for you further down the road with some of the other techniques you'll be learning.

We will start with something called square breathing. If you can count to four, you can do this. If you have a lot of breathing restriction, you can still do this. Anyone can do this. It is simple, easy to remember, and a great way to get your breath to slow down. It also gives your busy mind something to focus on that is not too complex but requires your attention, allowing it to quiet down quickly. You can think of this as the first thing you grab for in the Mindfulness Habit First Aid Kit.

I'll describe the steps. Read through the entire exercise first, and then practice them. Approach each step gently, patiently, and with a lot of compassion and self-acceptance. At the end, answer the questions in your journal.

⧗ Exercise 1-3: Square Breathing

This exercise is called *square breathing* because, like a square, it has four "sides." Also like a square, each of the four sides should be equal in length, so as you go, if you find it necessary for your comfort to shorten the length of one side, be sure to shorten them all so they remain the same.

To make sure that we're on the same page and you are able to follow what I'm talking about, when I say *the bottom of a breath* I mean the end of an exhale; when I say *the top of a breath*, I mean the end of an inhale.

Step One: Find a comfortable, upright, seated position. Just sit for a minute, letting yourself get settled. If it helps you to focus and concentrate, you can close your eyes. Let yourself breathe naturally for a couple of regular, relaxed breaths. When you are ready to start, and are *at the bottom* of one of your regular breaths, begin to inhale slowly, so that the inhalation part of your breath takes a moderate, even count of four for you to complete, and when you reach the count of four, you have taken in a nice, full breath.

Step Two: At the top of the inhale, at the end of the first count of four, you will hold your breath for an identical count of four. Just to make sure you're clear about what I am asking you to do, when I tell you to hold your breath, I am not saying you should hold your breath like you did when you were a kid, trying to see who could hold their breath the longest. It's more like you are suspending your breath where it is. Think about supporting your breath rather than gripping or restricting it.

Step Three: Gently let your breath out to a count of four, reaching a comfortable exhalation point at the end of the count where you just begin to feel a mild physical resistance. In this exercise, don't use the muscles in your ribs to forcefully push the air out of your lungs, but be sure to take your exhale all the way to a full and comfortable end. Remember, this square has four equal sides, so adjust to make sure that each count of four is the same length.

Step Four: Just as in Step Two, suspend your breath, holding your exhaled breath for another count of four.

Step Five: Start over with the in-breath. It is not uncommon to want to quickly grab your next inhale, breathing it in too quickly. If that happens to you, just continue with the rest of the pattern. Notice it; pay attention on your next breaths as they come up. You will realize that the feeling of panic about running out of air that causes you to do this is unfounded and unnecessary. You are fine and safe, and you'll relax into the pattern very quickly.

If you need to, feel free to take a break after a couple of cycles and let your breathing return to its natural depth and rate for a breath or two. Then you can begin a new cycle again.

Now practice the cycle a few times.

Good! I have no doubt that you have this figured out and will have no problems doing it on your own. This is easy-cheesy to learn, remember, and perform.

Now answer the questions having to do with your experience. This time for reflection on what you've practiced will give you more insight and help solidify your experience. It changes your whole relationship to what you are learning as you use more of your senses and learning styles to integrate the information.

Questions for Exercise 1-3

Take a second to get into your body. Read each question, close your eyes, and ask yourself the question, both in terms of what you *think* and how you *feel* in your body in response to the question, then record your answers and observations in your journal.

1. How did the square breathing feel?

2. How did you feel while you were doing it? How do you feel after doing it that is different than you felt before?

3. What was difficult? What was easy? What surprised you?

4. Is this something you can imagine being able to do on your own?

5. List two or three times, places, or situations where you can imagine doing this exercise.

6. How do you think you might benefit from this exercise?

7. Did you find this exercise:
   a. physically challenging?
   b. confusing?
   c. stimulated an emotional response?

Answering these questions is important. They help you stop and develop a richer relationship with what you are doing and how you are responding to it, and maybe even inspire an "aha!" moment.

Most importantly, they are another opportunity to connect with the moment, providing you with a greater sense of mindfulness.

⧖ Exercise 1-4: The Three-Part Breath

Here is another breathing exercise to learn. Like the first one, it has the benefit of increasing oxygen intake and feeding your cells, clearing your mind, and lifting your spirits. It also slows down and deepens your breathing pattern. This helps dispel feelings of anger, anxiety, and other strong emotions that cause you to lose focus and leave the moment.

This technique is called the three-part breath. This exercise is a bit more physical, but it is not difficult, and it is easy to customize it to your level of ability. Again, read through the instructions completely first, and be kind to yourself. You have permission for things to not be easy the first time. Do it anyway, trusting that you eventually will get better at it.

The biggest difference between square breathing and the three-part breath is that one is about a mindful, smooth regulation of depth and speed of the breath, and the other is about bringing a deeper attention to exploring and expanding the experience of breathing.

Sit in a comfortable, upright position, and bring your attention in to your body and breath. Think about the "breathing" areas of your torso as having three portions. The lowest portion is your belly, centered on your navel. The second area is the lower half of your ribs. Remember that you have ribs in the lower part of your rib cage that are below the breast bone, on the sides.

The last area is your upper half of your ribs, from about just below your armpits up to your collarbone—your top rib hides back behind it. You will be using these three areas of your body as focus for the next exercise. You don't need to be precise, only close and consistent in defining them.

Step One: You will begin, as we did before, with an exhale. Be sure to exhale as fully as you comfortably can.

Step Two: Focusing on the lower part of your breathing body, your belly area, breathe in, filling only that section of the body. Let it expand way out, while keeping the rest of your body neutral.

Step Three: Continue your inhale by breathing into the middle body (lower rib area), stacking your inhaled breath on top of the first part, your belly breath. Let your upper chest and shoulders remain neutral.

Step Four: Complete the inhale by extending your breath into your upper ribs, all the way up to the base of your throat. *Do not lift your shoulders.* Your entire torso should now be filled with air.

Step Five: Reverse the process to exhale, by exhaling the air from your belly, following with your middle torso, following with your upper chest. Be sure to treat each part of the exhale as separate, noting the distinction between each section. At the end of the last count of your exhale, you are back where you were when you began.

Step Six: Begin the process again from the beginning. After a couple of times, try to feather the edges of your breathing so that while the beginnings and endings of each breath or section of a breath remain distinct and separate, they flow into each other smoothly without feeling hard-edged or clunky.

Now answer the questions about your experiences with the three-part breath.

Questions for Exercise 1-4

1. How do you feel now that you've practiced the breathing exercises? Is it different than you felt before you started? How?

2. Is this something you can imagine being able to do on your own?

3. Was this easy or hard? If it was difficult, what about it did you have trouble with?

4. Was there anything in particular that you enjoyed or found pleasant?

5. Can you be patient and allow yourself to get better at doing it? If not, that's okay, but would you be willing to try coming back to it again later?

6. Under what circumstances can you imagine this exercise being useful? What would be the benefits?

Variations on the Three-Part Breath

Once you've had an opportunity to practice the three-part breath and get a sense for how it works, you might be interested in trying some variations.

VARIATION 1: REVERSE EXHALATION

This variation starts out exactly the same as the original three-part breath you learned, but it ends differently. Begin as before, with an exhale, followed by the same inhalation pattern, filling the three parts of your torso gently with air. But this time, when you exhale, you will *start at the upper ribs and work your way down through the lower ribs, with the belly coming last.*

Try the variation a few times. Do you notice a difference in how you feel when you begin the exhalations at the top of your body? Try both versions and see what you discover. I experience a distinct difference between the two (at least most of the time).

Your experience will of course be entirely yours, so just see what occurs to you as you practice this.

I have found that for me, exhaling from the top down makes me feel more grounded, where starting to exhale from the belly feels more energizing. Is this true for you?

Variation 2: Opening and Strengthening

This is a slightly more challenging version of the three-part breath. This variation is a bit more extreme, and requires more effort and concentration, but it's a very good thing to practice if your breathing muscles are chronically tight and your breathing tends to be shallow or restricted. It stretches, opens, and strengthens the muscles and tissue around your lungs and other muscles of respiration. This approach is a less "relaxing" version, but it can really slow down and open up your breathing when you feel angry, panicked, or experience other strong feelings.

Step One: You will begin, as we did before, with an exhale. Be sure to exhale as fully as you comfortably can.

Step Two: To a slow count of two, focusing on the lower part of your breathing body, your belly area, breathe in, filling only that section of the body. Let it expand way out, while keeping the rest of your body neutral.

Step Three: Continue to inhale by breathing into the middle body (lower rib area) to a count of two. Let your upper chest and shoulders remain neutral.

Step Four: Complete the inhale by breathing in to a count of two into your upper ribs, all the way up to the base of your throat. Do not lift your shoulders. Your entire torso should now be filled with air.

Step Five: Hold your inhaled breath to the same count of two.

Step Six: Reverse the process to exhale, by exhaling the air from your belly to a count of two, following with your middle torso, following with your upper chest. Be sure to make each section a separate count of two, noting the distinction between each section. At the end of the last count of two, you are back where you were when you began.

Step Seven: Hold the exhaled position for a count of two. Begin the process again from the beginning.

Try this on your own for a total of three or four times, then relax and let yourself have a few natural breaths. See if you can smooth out the breath while still being aware of the three separate parts of your body.

You may have found this difficult, but that means it's good for you to pay attention to the tension in those breathing muscles, give them some stretch, and gently open them up. Be patient with yourself; many people discover the limitations in their breathing when they first try this, but you will improve quickly. Becoming anxious will probably make it a little more difficult, so just do what you can and give yourself permission to be a beginner.

On the other hand, if you found this easy, you can increase how many of these you do, or you can stretch the length of the counts longer; just be sure to make them all the same length.

It takes practice to learn how to gauge your body's capacity for air inhalation and exhalation. I used to find that I would sometimes feel a bit panicky at the end, and have to resist the desire to begin inhaling too quickly and too stridently, quickly sucking all the air in at once. It didn't take too long for me to learn that my fear about running out of air was unnecessary and unfounded, and I was able to control my breath much better.

Chapter 1 Summary

Well, you've had a lot to think about.

Giving this process your energy and attention has far-reaching benefits, and I hope that you can trust in them enough to make the commitment to moving forward and trust that it will pay off.

I can understand if you feel like your motor is running and you want more, faster, louder, and longer, but there is a method to the way we are going into this. I am giving you what you can reasonably commit to given your time and energy, and, as you will learn in upcoming chapters, developing a habit is best done in a particular way. Blowing you right out of the gate will not benefit you in the long run.

So now, what do you think about what you've learned so far? Pretty straightforward, isn't it? That's the point. Nothing you're learning is terribly complicated. It can't be, because this needs to be information you can quickly grab from your toolbox and put right to work, wherever you are, at a moment's notice.

You'll notice that the two breathing exercises feel different, need a different quality of attention, and each one, from the outside, looks different from the other. There are lots of different techniques that you'll be learning, and there are a number of reasons for that, but it all boils down to the fact that you need a variety of approaches for different circumstances, places, moods, needs, problems, and learning styles. What works for you in your kitchen might not be appropriate when standing in line at the bank or driving your car.

You may be a person who responds well to starting things from the body, or you may be someone who needs to talk yourself through things first. Another variable is what you are experiencing when you need to come back to the present moment. It may be because you are feeling distracted, or it may be because you're feeling self-absorbed, or angry, or like you need support. All these variables mean that at different times, in different circumstances, you will need to determine what you find will work best for you, where you are, who you are, and what you're going through.

Things You've Learned in This Chapter

+ How this book is structured

+ How to make best use of the material in this book

+ Advantages of working with a group or partner

+ What stress is, and how worry, anxiety, and being overwhelmed can have a serious effect on your health

+ What meditation and mindfulness are, and what they are not

+ What preconceptions about them you may bring to your experience

+ How breathing is affected by the way you feel

+ That how you feel can be affected by your breathing

+ The square breathing technique

+ The three-part breath

Creating the Mindfulness Habit: Week 1
Practice

Practice a few repetitions of both square breathing and the three-part breath (including both variations) once each day for the first three days. Practice them mindfully, giving them your full attention for the duration of each one.

Take a moment before you begin each time and notice what you feel like, in general terms. You can use words like sad, bored, anxious, peaceful, sore, tired, relaxed, lively, etc., or you can use words like blue, fuzzy, shiny, flat—or make up your own (for example, "goinky" is a perfectly good word). Include noticing the state of your body—tense, fatigued, stiff, loose, etc. No judgment or analysis is needed, only noticing and accepting.

After practicing the breathing, notice how you feel. Do not make any attempt to analyze your feelings or sensations; just notice and acknowledge them. Notice how these techniques work for you and how you feel when you do them. This will become important when you start looking for the places where you might want to make use of them.

Each time you do the techniques, answer the following questions in your journal. The answers may very well change from day to day.

1. Which of the two breathing techniques was easier for you to do?

2. Do you prefer one over the other? Which one, and why?

3. What do you notice happening in your body when you do the square breathing?

4. What do you notice happening in your mind when you do the square breathing?

5. What do you notice happening in your body when you do the three-part breath?

6. What do you notice happening in your mind when you do the three-part breath?

After three days, you may continue to do both breath techniques and the variations, or just choose the one that appeals to you at the time for the remainder of the week. Pay attention to which one you choose, when you choose it, and (if you know) why you choose it, and record your experiences in your journal.

Habit Building

This next part is just as important, *if not more so*, than the previous task. This is the part where you work on making what you've learned fit into who you are, what you are doing, and where you are so that it becomes an integrated aspect of your lifestyle.

Get your journal, or your tablet, laptop, or phone, and set it up to record the following:

Begin to pay attention to times and places where it would be possible for you to use the techniques you learned in this lesson. It is okay if you think of them or notice them after the fact, even hours later. That's not only okay, it's good. Right now, we are beginning the process of forming habits, and the first step is to initiate new thoughts. In no time at all, you'll find yourself noticing these opportunities sooner and sooner.

Use your journal to make a record of these opportunities by recording the date and time of day that you would have used a technique. If you become aware of one of these opportunities in time to actually practice a technique, go for it! Then make a note of it, along with any changes in your body or mind that you notice after doing it.

Certainly, the goal is to eventually develop the connection between opportunity and action, but right now, creating the awareness is good practice and an important first step. It's also its own kind of mindfulness practice!

Keeping your journal pages solidifies the experiences in your mind and in your body. It might seem like it's unnecessary or extra work, but just focus on doing it for this week. Using these pages will really help you.

Have a great week.

Namaste.

CHAPTER 2

Week 2

The Mechanics of Habit Formation

Welcome to Week 2. I hope you had a wonderful and interesting week.

Did you take the time to do the habit formation assignments? If you made any effort at all, I want to congratulate you. Please, please, please don't get discouraged, frustrated, or angry with yourself. In the first week, even just remembering to remember can be an exercise in and of itself! You have to begin somewhere. The goal of using the journal is not to use it forever (unless you decide you want to); it's to help you through this practice of developing your habit of bringing yourself back to the present moment.

I want to look at why taking the time to do the exercises can support you and what they can help you accomplish. In the first week, I mentioned that my goal is for you to not only share a set of techniques that can help you be more mindful and take some of the stress out of your everyday life, but to give you what you need in order to make using them a habit.

So let's take a moment to talk about how habits work. The formation of a habit is the process of making certain behaviors become automatic. Some habits are good: brush your teeth, put your dirty clothes in the hamper, look both ways before crossing the street. Others, maybe not so much: a cookie at the bakery every time you go grocery shopping, a cigarette with your coffee...you know what these look like.

We talk a lot about breaking bad habits but not so much about making good ones. The process of doing either is made easier when you have an understanding of how habits work.

Habits have distinct parts to them. The first part is the thought (I want a cookie), the second is the action (I walk to the bakery and buy a cookie), and the third is the reward (I eat the cookie).

In our case, the habit you want to create is one of becoming mindful and present, quieting the mind, especially in situations of worry or distress.

The parts of the habit you are trying to create look something like this:

+ Seeing and recognizing opportunities to be present and mindful (the thought)

+ Doing something that brings you into the present moment (the action)

+ Becoming present, calm, peaceful, alert—feeling good, focused, and free from your distress (the reward)

It has also been shown that forming new habits works best when they are first broken down into small, bite-sized segments, are specific in their intent, and are achieved by following a clear plan. The set of weekly tasks I've laid out for you is designed to be a reflection of those ideal factors for habit formation.

Let's look at the weekly habit formation practice you were given at the end of the last lesson as an example. You were asked to begin noticing opportunities where you could integrate the breathing exercises you had just learned into your daily life. How well does this follow these rules? First of all, the expectation of what you need to do is very simple and requires no special equipment or environment. This makes it easy and accessible. It is something that you can reasonably fit into your schedule and doesn't require any special time set aside, and the task is clearly defined. I wanted it to be something that you can readily achieve—a small, bite-sized task.

Another part of your assignment for developing your new habit was to practice the breathing exercises. So how does this facilitate you forming a new habit? There are a couple of good things here. First of all, you begin to learn the breathing. This builds connections in your nervous system and actually creates new neural pathways. It's like wearing a rut in the road. The benefit of this is that, over time, it allows these actions to come more naturally and without a lot of concentration. It's like practicing your backhand over and over in tennis, or learning your scales at the piano.

You are also experiencing that there is a connection between that activity (breathing exercises) and the reward (increased oxygen, slowed respiration, release of muscle tension, and increased sense of calm). In other words, you begin to show your subconscious that deep breathing = feeling good, yet another pathway you are making in your brain. Now you have your reward, the ability to connect taking a moment to be more present with changing how you feel for the better.

The reward feeds another important aspect of habit formation, the craving. As you begin to anticipate the rewards that come with your actions, you are increasingly motivated to seek out opportunities to practice them. That wanting and seeking out ways and opportunities is the craving. This brings you back to the beginning, the first part of the habit, the thought, because now you have part of you that remembers that you liked what you were doing, that what you felt was rewarding. Reinforce this with what I asked you to do in your first habit formation assignment—noticing opportunities to practice mindfulness techniques.

When you break it down like this, you can see that habits are cycles that reinforce themselves. Establishing them, making the connections, and developing all the choices and an awareness of them as opportunities takes time and wholehearted commitment.

I think that understanding this process, its parts, and how it works will help you understand the reason for the habit formation assignments, and motivate you to continue practicing and devoting time to them.

Fleeing the Tiger: The Physical Expression of Stress

It's time to look more deeply into your mind's relationship with your body and your body as a pathway toward quieting your mind.

As you saw in the breathing we worked with in the previous chapter, the relationship between what you're thinking or feeling and what your body is experiencing can be immediate, direct, and powerful.

Things can leave you breathless or with butterflies in your tummy. Events can be a pain in the neck, make your heart beat faster, or cause you to grit your teeth.

We looked at the body as a reflection of your emotional state a little bit when we worked with breathing, but your breath is only one of the ways your mental and emotional states are expressed in your body, changing how it feels and how it behaves.

When you looked at your breath, you also saw that changing your body changes how you experience things. Maybe you saw how things seem to slow down, your vision opens up, and you literally see things more clearly. Your body gets more oxygen and the slower rate of respiration can begin to defuse the body mechanisms that are related to the fight-or-flight response, changing your focus, beginning to reduce some of the fear-based responses, allowing you to think more clearly. Along with this you will see that there is an improvement and normalization of your digestion, and you will let go of excess muscle tone and tension so that you feel less jumpy.

This is because these physical responses are some of the many, many things that are set in motion when you find yourself in a situation that provokes that fight-or-flight response I mentioned before. It is actually an amazing adaptation for survival. Like so many aspects of our bodies, it is a thing of genius and beauty.

The fight-or-flight response is a complex cascade of physiological actions that have an impact on every system in your body. In preparation for fleeing that saber-toothed tiger, your body shoots a lot of different chemicals into your system that cause a whole bunch of physiological responses. Your breathing changes and your heart speeds up to increase the delivery of oxygen to your muscles. There is more fuel released by your liver and that gets delivered too. But the parts of the body that get this fuel and oxygen to burn are your extremities, the parts you need for running and climbing. Your digestion gets shut down, as do reproductive functions. After all, these are not very important when you are running for your life.

You get tunnel vision as the peripheral vision closes off to focus your sight on what is directly in front of you. You perspire more to keep your body cool, your mouth gets dry, and your bladder relaxes and your bowels loosen to vacate your body for decreased weight and increased mobility. Your muscle tone increases to allow for quicker response and greater strength, and your blood-clotting agents go into overtime to staunch blood flow in case of injury.

When the danger is past, the body is designed to replace this fight-or-flight response with a relaxation response, sometimes called "rest-and-digest." This response essentially undoes everything that happened during the crisis. It's the reason that after an emergency or perceived danger, like a car accident, you get all wobbly or your knees go weak, and you feel like you can't stand up as the tone of your muscles decreases suddenly and dramatically.

This response is great when it works, but the problem is that so many of the things in our lives that we now view as threats never completely go away; you can't outrun your mortgage payment, for example. So when the sense of threat never quite leaves completely, the relaxation response never gets a chance to kick in.

The result of this is that you live with part of your physiology always turned on in a mode that is designed for only short bursts of time, just enough for you to get yourself out of immediate danger. The stuff that your body does in situations of danger is not a healthy norm for the other 98 percent of your life. You now are operating with the physical symptoms of stress, which include incomplete digestion, increased muscle tension, thickened blood, narrowed vision, a heart that is working overtime…well, you can see where this is going.

Adjusting your breathing is a way of using your body to shift itself to a place that facilitates both it and your mind being quieter and more mindful. It is a way to acknowledge and shift your relationship to your experience, making a good first step toward letting go of that leftover fear response, bringing you into the present, and giving your body a chance to go back to rest-and-digest.

Now you are going to practice another way of using your body in a mindful way that places your attention on a more comprehensive way of experiencing your body. You are going to practice mindful standing, or standing meditation. You'll start tuning in to your body for opportunities to focus your attention.

Giving yourself a place to rest your attention goes a long way toward quieting your mind, and you don't want that place to be complicated or busy. This practice is simple, but it has enough layers to hold your attention. Although it may not seem so at first, it can be endlessly fascinating and absorbing. It will become one of your favorite go-to ways of reconnecting with the present moment.

Learning how to do a standing meditation will give you a wonderfully flexible skill that you can find many opportunities to practice, so keep your eyes open for times and places you can sneak this one in.

If you are familiar with yoga, what you will be doing is very much like *tadasana*, or mountain pose. It is a way of standing that is deliberate, yet relaxed. It requires that you give it a certain degree of constant attention in order to maintain a proper posture. This means that you get the benefit not only of quieting your body, but you are also learning another way of quieting the mind by keeping your attention on a simple focus.

Again, as in the previous exercises, read through the instructions once or even a couple of times to get clear about what you're going to be doing before you try it.

⏳ Exercise 2-1: Standing Meditation

You may choose to practice this with shoes or without. Try it both ways if you'd like, and see what you notice. Some people like to close their eyes because it allows them to feel like they can really focus, but you may find it hard to maintain your balance if you do. If you are feeling tippy, open your eyes and allow them to have a soft focus so you are not looking specifically at anything. Or, if you find this hard as well, give yourself a single point of focus, some sort of unmoving object like a crack in the floor or a fold in the curtain or a corner of a picture frame. You don't want anything complex or too visually interesting.

Stand up and, if you'd like, shift your weight slightly left and right to feel that you're making a connection between your feet and the ground, and to get yourself feeling more balanced and centered.

Feel all the edges of your feet where they are in contact with the ground. Imagine your feet are making a clear, clean footprint.

Stand with your legs straight, but do not lock your knees. Think of having a "micro bend" in your knees, or just think of your legs having a relaxed feeling. Your legs should feel a balance between relaxed and active.

Let your shoulders drop away from your ears as much as they can without pushing them or forcing them. Let the pull of gravity on your arms allow your shoulders to drop naturally. Do not roll them forward or back, just drop.

Visualize your body as a series of bones connecting and supporting each other smoothly and naturally from the ground all the way up your spine. Imagine your head balanced perfectly at the top of your spine. Now feel that there is a hook on the very top of your head, and that attached to that hook is a string that is gently helping to suspend you from the sky, so that you are perfectly balanced between your connection to the ground and the force of gravity, and the tension of the string pulling gently upward through you from the top of your head. Feel long through the back of your neck.

Let your face relax. Notice any tension in your brow, around your eyes, your jaw, and your mouth. Breathe naturally. Pay attention to your body, checking in with your feet and their connection to the ground, checking your shoulders to be sure they are not inching up toward your ears, and feeling the gentle alignment of your head and spine.

Take notice of what it feels like to just stand here. Let this be where your attention rests for a couple of minutes. Make any small adjustments that you need to in order to maintain your posture.

Bring your attention to a general sense of being in your body, of maintaining the balance between striving and ease as it comes into alignment, and let it stay there.

Anytime you find your mind starting to drift or notice it starting to get noisy, analytical, judgmental, or busy, check back in with your body, and run through the alignment and the sense of being balanced in space. Do this as many times and as often as necessary to keep your attention on your sense of standing. Stay here as long as is comfortable.

Now, go to your journal, and please answer the following questions about your experience.

Questions for Exercise 2-1

1. How did it feel to just stand, and to stand with a focused, mindful attention?

2. What did you notice about your body?

3. Did you notice any difference between how you felt before you did this and the way you felt afterward? If so, what was it?

4. What did you like about it?

5. Did you notice if your breathing or other physical symptoms changed? If so, how?

6. What places or circumstances can you imagine using this in your daily life?

Congratulations, you now have learned a technique for focusing and quieting the body and the mind. What you have learned lays a great foundation for moving your ability to be present out into the world, giving you more and more opportunities for being able to find places for promoting a sense of calm, and taking a tiny but important break from the craziness of life.

The Senses

With the lessons you have learned so far, you've been using your body as an important touchstone to bring you into a state of being present through your breathing or by maintaining your posture.

There are other gifts that come with having a body that are also very helpful in bringing your mind into focus and grounding it in the present. Your five wonderful senses can go into the have-at-all-times, go-everywhere tool bag along with your breathing.

There is nothing like them for bringing your attention to a single focus, and your mind to a quiet place in the present moment.

Using one of your senses as a source for opportunities to focus your attention has great benefits. They are already part of your experience, so there is very little "learning curve" for using them and it feels very easy and straightforward. This also means they are infinitely adaptable to almost any occasion or setting, making them an easy place to go to first.

But don't make the mistake of believing that their common, everyday nature and easy access make them second best. Your senses are a powerful force; they are the reason that our species has survived, and they have a direct pathway to the brain. They are my go-to more often than not when I need to quickly jerk back to the present moment.

Using the senses as ways of focusing your attention has both pros and cons. Your senses are so rich that experiencing even just one of them at a time can be very intense and complex. This means that the experience can be fraught with possibilities for your mind to wander off as you are inspired to consider, analyze, remember, reminisce, or evaluate your experiences with them, finding yourself dragged out of the present moment.

However, it also means that experiencing one of your senses in the moment can be an ever-changing celebration of being alive, filled with information that can't help but bring you into the lavishness of the magical here and now.

If using the senses is so great, and so fundamental, why didn't we begin with it? As you may know, the simplest of things have hidden layers, and the seemingly uncomplicated may have a depth and complexity of experience that you can spend a lifetime exploring. Once you bring your attention completely to experiencing one of your senses, it's like opening a door into an entirely new world.

This world has doorways into memories, ideas, thoughts, realizations, and opinions, and that's where it gets tricky. Within the simplicity is also an opportunity for your mind to start creating connections, stories, analysis, and monologues. Bringing your attention back, over and over again, to your experience in the present becomes more important, and something that you can spend the rest of your life working with. It was good to get a little practice with something more physical and less mentally and emotionally loaded before you give this a try.

I don't say this to scare you off but to encourage you! It's not that this will be an overwhelming experience—it will be one that continues to reveal itself in new and interesting ways over time. This will never get boring.

When you bring your senses into use as a focus for your attention, you start to experience opinions, feelings, and attitudes about what is going on around you. This feels good/bad; this taste is pleasant/unpleasant; this sound is soothing/irritating. You begin to crave the things that you label as pleasing and feel a need to move to avoid those that you label as unpleasant. Experiencing strong preferences is another way your mind becomes agitated and creates the kind of discomfort that can contribute to feelings of stress.

But don't see this as a problem, because really, this is a great opportunity! Why is that? It's a chance to develop the ability to notice your preferences and then to keep from getting caught up in them. It is nice to be able to notice when we are getting worked up about the things we don't like, and dissatisfied by wanting more of the things we do. Having that realization is a powerful wake-up call. Reality cares little for your preferences, so creating a lot of energy, drama, and distraction around them is often a frustrating—and therefore stressful—exercise in futility. Exploring your senses will begin to give you some insight into this.

Note well, your mind *will* do all of these things I have mentioned. It will make connections, exert preferences, tell stories. How do I know? Because you are human, incarnate, and living. It is inevitable—and it's okay. Please don't allow it to frustrate you; you're doing great. I promise.

I also promise you will enjoy this. It's really, really cool. You'll see.

⏳ Exercise 2-2: Sense of Touch

The sense you'll work with in this lesson is your sense of touch. The sense of touch can be a quick and powerful way to instantly bring you into the moment. The exploration you'll be practicing now is an elaborate one, and will give you a rich introduction into the power of touch to bring you into the present moment, but it doesn't need to be this involved when you use it during your day.

Begin by getting yourself into a comfortable position, preferably an upright seated or standing position. This will help you stay awake and present. Take a couple of deep, relaxed breaths, and then let your breathing return to its natural depth and rate. Close your eyes.

Take your hand and place it on top of the other hand, gently running it over the surface, feeling the texture and contours. Let your experience be one of pure touch, noticing any tendency to judge, label, or describe what you're feeling. When you notice this happening, acknowledge it, let it go, and bring your attention back to the sense of touch.

Let your fingers notice the texture of your hand, and then, if you'd like, try switching your focus so your hand is noticing what it is like to be touched by your fingers. Don't lose track of the moment.

Let your hand travel up your arm, feeling the texture of your arm, your sleeve, the folds of fabric, the texture of the fabric under your fingers and how it feels against your skin. Let your other hand do the same on your other arm, letting them follow your arms up to your shoulders. Feel the shape and solidity of your shoulders.

Bring your hands to your neck, feeling the shape of your throat, and around the back of your neck to your hairline. Allow yourself to have your neck also feel the touch of your hands on your skin. Let your hands run up onto your scalp and through your hair, feeling its texture, its density, its length. Run your fingers through the length of your hair.

Remember that if you find yourself judging (my hair is too fine), analyzing (I could really use a haircut), or thinking in any way that takes your attention off of your sense of touch, to just notice that you've done so and bring your attention back to your fingers and hands.

Touch your ears, feeling their shape, and also letting your ears feel what it is like to be touched. Lastly, let your fingers explore your face, its shape and texture, its resilience and softness. Touch your eyes, your cheeks, the shape of your nose, and the texture of your lips.

Now let your hands rest, and allow yourself to just sit for a moment, noticing how you feel in your body. Then you might also notice what your mind is like. Don't get caught in analyzing or making a list; just quietly observe for a moment and see what rises to the front of your awareness.

Open your eyes, grab your journal, and go to the questions for Exercise 2-2 and answer them.

Questions for Exercise 2-2
In your journal, answer the following questions about the experience you just had. Please be assured that there are no right or

wrong answers. Be gentle with yourself and accept that wherever you are is okay.

1. When you checked in at the end, did you feel the same or different compared to how you felt before you started? If it was different, how?

2. What are some ways that you could vary this exercise for different occasions?

3. Name some places where that you could do this and how you might do it.

4. How might practicing this be helpful to you?

5. Did you learn anything about your body, what it's doing, or what it needs? What did you learn?

6. What part of this exercise did you like? What part did you dislike? Why?

Variation on the Sense of Touch

The approach you learned above was a series of tactile experiences based upon touching your body and experiencing touch that way. This variation is a good one for such public places as your workplace.

Grab an object that is handy and close your eyes. Start by running your fingertips lightly over the surface of the object, getting a sense of the general shape and an initial impression of the surface texture. After you've done that for as long as you like, let your fingers find a place of interest to explore further. Let your fingertips follow the shape and texture of that place until they are led to the next place. Explore that one until you find yourself moving on to the next one. Continue with this until you feel like you are ready to be finished.

This exercise can take you quite deep into your experience of touch surprisingly quickly, as you discover the most mundane of objects anew, and quiet and refresh your mind.

Chapter 2 Summary

Sometimes people make an appointment with me in order to address their pain, and when they arrive they tell me that either that morning or the night before a whole bunch of things started hurting. Sometimes they ask things like, "Do you think my body knew I was coming to see you, and was telling me what it wanted worked on?"

I have been known to answer with something along the lines of "I don't see *how* your body could *possibly* know; I mean you carry your brain around in a suitcase all day, right?" Then they laugh, sometimes a bit self-consciously, as they realized how much they have, in their imagination, separated their mind and body, and they also see how little that reflects the reality of how things really are.

You now have a deeper understanding of why your body feels the way it does under stress, and you can also understand that providing a space that takes you out of fight-or-flight mode is healthy for your body. You can use your body to quiet your body *and* your mind, and quieting the mind also quiets the body. They are all the same thing.

You are now learning some ways of doing things that are going to be more challenging. They are challenging because they will cause you to be more aware of your busy, busy mind. This is good! Noticing your busy mind and then practicing letting all those busy thoughts go by is an important way of being in the moment.

Please don't let yourself get frustrated. Believe me when I tell you that even the most experienced practitioners of mindfulness continually have to notice when their mind becomes busy and bring it back to the present moment.

Things You've Learned in This Chapter

+ The parts that make up a habit and the steps required in order to form new ones

+ What the fight-or-flight response is and what it does to your body

+ What the relaxation or rest-and-digest response is

+ How when you are under stress you are living in a constant, low-grade version of the fight-or-flight response

- The standing meditation technique

- How working with the senses helps you see and possibly let go of preference and judgment

- How practicing with the senses activates more mental and emotional distractions than some of the previous activities, and that they require a concentrated level of vigilance in order to keep in the moment

- Working with a focus on your sense of touch as a way of staying in the present moment

Creating the Mindfulness Habit: Week 2
Practice, Part 1

Practice one of the breathing activities you learned in Week 1 four times this week. Practice it mindfully, giving it your full attention for the duration of your practice. Make notes about your experiences in your journal.

Practice, Part 2

Practice the standing meditation every day this week. You can do it for as long or short a period of time as you choose. Try mixing it up, and pay attention to what happens when you practice doing this for different lengths of time and in different moods, circumstances, and environments.

Keep notes in your journal, reflecting on each time you practice it, and each time answer the following questions. It is entirely possible that the answers will change from day to day.

1. What are you noticing while you are doing the standing meditation?

2. What about it is easy? What is difficult?

3. Are the difficult things getting easier as you practice it more?

4. What do you dislike about this exercise?

5. What other places might you use this as a mindfulness technique in your day?

Practice, Part 3

As many times as you have the opportunity to do so, do the meditation on touch. It does not have to be elaborate or follow the formula we used exactly; you can use it as an inspiration. Keep track in your journal:

1. When did you choose to do the meditation on touch?

2. What did you notice?

3. As you practiced it over time, what changed?

4. Now that you've done it a couple of times, name a few ways you could integrate this into your life.

Habit Building

Continue to actively look for times and places where it would be possible for you to use the techniques you have learned so far. It is okay if you think of them or notice them after the fact, even hours later, but you are probably beginning to become aware of them sooner—maybe it's even been in the moment when it is happening.

It has only been a week or so since you started, so be sure to be gentle with yourself and not look for huge changes to be revealed right away. You are still early in the process of forming those habits.

Again, use your journaling pages to make notes recording when opportunities arise. Are you catching these opportunities in time to use these techniques? If you have, that's great; be sure to make note of any changes in your body or mind that you notice after doing them. You have a few tools now, and some understanding of how they work and what happens when you use them. If you stopped right now, you'd still have some really valuable things to move forward with.

The changes that you allow to develop over time, without being forced or rushed, are the ones that you integrate best; they are the ones that hang around. Enjoy what you are learning. Enjoy the moment. Be present and patient.

I believe in you.

Namaste.

CHAPTER 3

Week 3

Demystifying Meditation

Welcome back! We are now on Week 3 of creating the Mindfulness Habit and finding the space for a calm, quiet mind in your life.

As we go through these weeks, some of the things you will be learning are ways of being more present in what you are doing, or where you are being, no matter what or where they are. They are focused specifically on mindfulness. Some of these are meditations—in other words, specific, intentional acts that exercise your mindfulness muscles by using them to focus and quiet the mind.

These meditation techniques will be useful to you for a number of reasons. They have a physical, active component that centers them in the body for a quick grounding in the present. They are all particularly well suited for you to implement as part of other activities you do throughout the day, especially those two to ten minutes of "dead time" where you have to be someplace, but you can't really be *doing* anything. And very importantly, they teach you something that will help you lay a foundation for each next step in practicing being more and more completely present. The way we are using meditation should not feel excessive, extra, or special.

The meditations you will be learning can be characterized by the following:

+ Allowing your mind to be alert and attentive

+ Allowing your mind to be calm, focused, and concentrated without strain

+ An increased awareness of the world around you

+ Being in the moment; not worrying about the past or future

+ A process more than a goal; a beautiful, inspiring journey rather than a destination

As much as it is good to know what meditation *is*, it is also good to clarify any confusion about what you are doing by telling you that the following *do* not characterize the meditations you will be practicing:

+ Falling asleep (being in the present requires you to be *awake* to it)

- Going into a trance (this is characterized by a shift *out* of the richness of the moment)

- Daydreaming (daydreaming is good for you, but it needs its own time and place)

- Shutting off from reality or your surroundings (you are trying to be more in tune, not less)

- Becoming lost in thought or disconnecting from where you are (self-explanatory, I would think)

- Self-hypnosis (this is a deeply internal but very disconnected state)

None of the things on the second list are bad or wrong in and of themselves. They all have their uses. But they are all things that crop up often when people are trying to shift their mind to a state of being present, and none of them is what we are trying to achieve with these efforts. They can easily cause a lot of confusion when you are first learning to practice mindfulness.

It makes no difference which category you choose to put each technique into, or how you personally choose to define them. The best thing to do is practice, practice, practice whatever you're learning.

It is possible that after you've developed the Mindfulness Habit, you might decide that you want to go deeper and start a more rigorous meditation practice, taking your mind to a new level of insight and quiet. Maybe what you learn in this book will be enough for you and you will be satisfied with making your days easier, your transitions smoother, your mind more open, and your heart more gentle by just remembering to come back into the present moment in all its wonder.

For now, working with developing the Mindfulness Habit will go very far toward quieting your mind and providing a space for calm, restoration, and peace for you every day.

The next thing you'll be doing is a meditation. It is a walking meditation, and it is a very old, traditional approach to bringing meditation and mindfulness into movement. It is traditionally thought of as a way to take those characteristics of mindfulness and presence you practice when sitting in meditation out into the world you walk around in.

The way it often works for me is that it's more like a bridge between the inner world and the outer world, and the traffic can go either direction. I find the world to be a very fertile environment for me to find opportunities to be in the present moment and therefore a good place for me to quiet my mind. Because of this, I tend to find walking meditation to be a bridge from the outer to the inner world of quiet.

The walking meditation makes a great example for understanding the distinction between mindful activity and meditation. You can walk mindfully, or you can do walking meditation.

Both are valuable, both create a mindful state, but they are distinctly different.

The first option, walking mindfully, is taking something that you are already doing, like walking to the library, but doing it with an increased level of attention to your actions and your surroundings. On the other hand, walking meditation is something that you do for its own sake, setting it aside as a separate activity.

I know that I promised you stuff that you can integrate into your daily life, not anything that you need to set aside special time for, but trust me on this one. First of all, I will show you that this is something that you can find a little space for without it being an extra task, so don't worry too much about that. Second, practicing this is an important intermediary step in being able to take your mindful activity to the next level.

Remember the steps of habit formation? Specific, simple, achievable steps are key, and keeping the focus on one thing at a time will keep you from getting overwhelmed, distracted, or frustrated.

We'll start and you'll see what I mean.

⏳ Exercise 3-1: Walking Meditation

You will need some space to do this technique—a minimum of about eight to ten feet of uninterrupted space is ideal, but if pressed, you can do it with less. It is best to first learn this without shoes, either barefoot or in socks, so that you can really connect with the ground. Later, after you are more comfortable and connected with it, you can do it in shoes if you like. If you are someone who must wear shoes for reasons of comfort or safety, that is fine; you can learn it that way too. Remember, I am a firm believer in meeting you where you are right now, and helping you be okay with that. I want you to be comfortable and confident with yourself, no matter what happens.

As with all the exercises in this book, before you begin, read the instructions through once.

Begin by taking a moment to be in standing meditation position, shoulders relaxed, feet solidly in contact with the ground, head balanced comfortably on top of your spine, feeling balanced, relaxed, and alert. Feel your face relax. Breathe naturally.

You are going to begin walking very slowly. Your steps will be short, and each one will move through space at the rate that allows you to really pay attention to your experience, roughly one step per second.

When you begin, you will pick up your first foot, feeling each part of your foot leave its contact with the ground, and then gently put it down, rolling it back down from your heel, until your foot is flat on the ground, being aware of it coming gradually into contact with the surface below it. Then lift your other foot off the ground, feeling it slowly breaking its contact, moving through space, and then connecting with the ground.

The most important thing to do is to notice and acknowledge your walk as it is. Noticing your foot's relationship to the ground, and then to the air, and your body's relationship to gravity and your feet, are the things that should hold your attention.

Now I want you to begin, lifting, moving, stepping; lifting, moving, stepping. Continue on with this until you reach the end of your walking space. At that point, with the same sort of mindful attention, turn, and walk back to where you began.

Feel free to repeat this if you'd like.

The incidental benefits of practicing this kind of walking are that it can result in improved balance, better posture, and healthier joints. As you pay more attention to how you walk, and your awareness increases, you may want to see if you can avoid what I call "Frankenstein walking." This is when people lift their foot, and then fall onto it, flat-footed, making them lurch like an old-movie Frankenstein's monster.

This is not inherently bad; it's just that there are a couple of reasons to avoid doing this. The first is that you are not getting the opportunity to enjoy the full potential of this experience. If you notice you are doing this more lurching style of walking, see if you can make your movements a little smoother and notice more about your contact between the parts of your foot and the floor. Another reason is that this a bad habit to get into; it is better to be walking, not falling forward and catching yourself.

You may be doing this because when you lift your foot and are briefly standing on only one foot, you are having trouble balancing and feel like you are tilting or wobbling. Here's something you can try that's just a good tip for balancing. It comes from my tai ji teacher.

Think of your body in halves: upper half and lower half, and left half and right half. At any given time, you need to have a balance of "substantial" and "insubstantial" throughout the halves; otherwise you fall over.

When your left leg (for example) is off the ground, it becomes entirely insubstantial and the right leg becomes entirely substantial—*on the lower half of your body*. You can balance this by thinking about compensating on the *upper* half of your body. So, if your left leg is off the ground, think about the left side of your upper body as being more substantial to compensate and you will feel balanced.

If this is just too complicated, confusing, or unnecessary for you, *don't worry about it*. This is just a tip that many students have found useful. If you don't find it to be so, then it's not for you, and that's okay.

When I find myself getting too caught up in worrying about being "technique-y," I put the mental brakes on and then mentally repeat to myself, "Just walk," and I do. It is more important to be mindful of what it is that you are doing than worrying about doing it "right." Whatever you are experiencing in the moment is what you should observe.

When you are done practicing your walking meditation, answer the following questions in your journal.

Questions for Exercise 3-1

1. How did you feel about the walking meditation? What did you like or dislike about it?

2. What about it was difficult?

3. Did you have an "aha!" or revelation about mindful movement and your body?

4. Obviously, this is not something you can do just anywhere. I understand that this kind of super-slow movement can appear a bit odd, but I also know that there are some opportunities to try it. List as many of them as you can.

Variations on Walking Meditation

VARIATION 1

If you are really enjoying going deeply into the walking meditation, or you'd like to make it something that draws even more of your attention and focus, try this addition to your practice.

When walking, coordinate your steps to your breathing. Coordinate the movement of your foot lifting from the floor and leaving the ground with breathing in, and as it moves toward returning to the ground, begin to breathe out. Keep your breath even and be sure to "feather" the edges of your breath so that it is a natural, smooth breath that follows your particular natural pattern and rhythm at this particular time and place. Your breathing should not be exaggerated or abrupt, just a natural in and out breath that you follow with your steps.

Variation 2

Another variation is to imagine that as you gradually connect your foot with the ground, and your weight begins to shift, you feel that foot, and then the leg, fill with substance, chi, life force, whatever you like. Then, as you put down the other foot, you feel that one fill as that sense of energy or substance flows from the first foot into the second, until it feels like the energy is pumping back and forth through your body. This is based on martial arts techniques, and can really feel great as you move your awareness back and forth through your body, energizing it completely.

I believe that everyone has a great opportunity to do walking meditation in their home right now. Any trip between any two rooms (unless you live in a giant mansion of a home) can be partly or entirely done as a walking meditation. Going to the kitchen for a drink? Walking meditation. Need to head to the bathroom to brush your teeth? There you go.

Most importantly, the skills for being more mindful in movement are going to serve you well in the upcoming weeks, so practice this now, and if after this week you don't use it again, you will still have gotten something crucial out of it.

The Senses: Hearing

When you use something as a place to rest your attention, we call it an anchor. Think about a boat and how when you want it to stay in one place, you drop the anchor. When wind, currents, and waves come along and influence the boat, the anchor is the thing that keeps the boat from drifting away. The boat can bob and float a bit, but the anchor gently tugs it back before it goes very far.

Think of your mind as being the boat. As you've noticed by now, your mind can drift away very easily, only instead of wind and waves taking it away from a still place, it is thoughts—memories, ideas, analysis, judgment, or planning and organizing thoughts. Just as an anchor prevents the waves from taking a boat away from the place it is anchored, *your* anchor keeps your mind from drifting off on waves of thinking.

Besides what you've learned so far, another anchor available for your use is your sense of hearing.

No matter how quiet the room is, there is something to hear. In my city, there is a room that is specially created to be the quietest room in the world, and even in that room, you can still hear something. You can hear your body making its sounds—breathing, digestion, heartbeat. What this means is that you can use this mindfulness technique anywhere, whether where you are is noisy or quiet. It all works the same way.

You can imagine the wonderful flexibility of this exercise. It is useful almost any time and any place. It also has a wonderful capacity to really quiet and focus your mind, while challenging you to remain outside the place of thought and analysis. And it is something that you can do without moving around, while seated or standing, with your eyes open or closed.

Practicing this can also provide you with the ability to be in a lovely place of total presence, free from the need to label or build a story around what you hear. You can enter into a state of openness and acceptance around your environment that is very peaceful.

However, you might develop an awareness of how you respond to certain sounds as you judge them as good or bad, pleasant or unpleasant. Be aware of these feelings and reactions if you notice them, and notice any sensations that you experience along with these qualities of wanting more of the good ones, and pushing away the bad ones. Don't dwell on these responses. Just as with each of the techniques you've learned thus far, observe your thoughts and reactions, and then come back to the anchor.

When you practice this, notice how you feel when you can let go of the tendency to crave something you find pleasant, or to step out of judgment and irritation in your relationship to those things you may find unpleasant. There are great lessons here.

This is one of my personal favorites. I feel like the world is an orchestra playing a wild and improvisational symphony that will never be repeated. It makes a moment feel very special to me.

To get the most out of it, read through this entire exercise before beginning.

⧗ Exercise 3-2: The Sense of Hearing

Consider setting a timer for five minutes before beginning to practice this exercise. It will allow you to put your full attention on what you are doing, relieving your mind from the burden of wondering how long you have been doing it.

Begin by getting yourself into a comfortable position, preferably an upright, seated position. This will help you stay awake and present. Take a couple of deep, relaxed breaths, and then let your breathing return to its natural depth and rate. Close your eyes to help you limit your attention to your sense of hearing.

Just sit quietly for a moment until you feel like you are ready to be fully present. Then think to yourself, "What am I hearing right now?" Quietly wait for the sounds to reveal themselves. Allow your sense of hearing to open up and let the sounds find their way in.

Your experience of listening will be different from one time to the next. One time, noises may all rush in as one sound and then begin to separate into distinctly different sounds. They may reveal themselves in layers or individual notes. These notes or sounds may blend together into something almost musical, or they may move back and forth, into and out of the foreground individually. There is no particular way that it should unfold for you, and how it unfolds will probably be different each time you practice this.

There will be a strong tendency to label or analyze the sounds, or to categorize them by quality, such as loud, soft, natural, mechanical, good, bad. When this starts to happen, just notice it, and then return to the sense of being open to the sounds. Experience them washing over and through you, rising and falling, coming and going, without judging them or naming them.

Each time you find that you have had a sound spark a thought or feeling, just acknowledge that it has occurred, and then bring your attention back to a sense of being present with the sounds around you. It is expected and natural that this should happen, so don't be hard on yourself when it does; only notice and let it go.

Now use your journal to record your responses to the following questions.

Questions for Exercise 3-2

1. What did you hear? How did sounds reveal themselves to you?

2. What did you like about this? What did you find most difficult about it?

3. How do you feel after practicing this? Do you feel different than you felt before you began? How?

4. Name two or more circumstances in which you could find opportunities to use this in your life.

Chapter 3 Summary

Not all meditation requires you to sit silently facing a wall. The things you've learned, whether you call them meditations, mindfulness exercises, or anything else, have been chosen to be simple, easily understood, and quickly accessed.

As you become more practiced at quieting the mind, you will notice that creating that space allows for lots of room for thoughts to rush in. It is important to do three things: always stay open to the realization that your attention has been hijacked by your thoughts; be aware of being fooled into thinking you are being mindful, when in fact, you are in a state of sleepiness, daydreaming, or other drifty, non-present state; and most importantly, be patient and gentle with yourself. The need to constantly bring your attention back to your body, your movement, your hearing, or your touch is part of this process. If you aren't bringing your attention back regularly and often, it's probably *not* because you are so present; it is probably because you are not.

Pay careful attention to how much your mind quiets, your attention shifts, and your body responds as you begin to include these techniques in your repertoire. The ability to be more present will allow you to be more aware of the presence of preference and your response to preferences. This can help you see that how you respond to these preferences can cause or relieve feelings of stress.

Your sense of hearing is a wonderful, easily accessed, and powerful tool for bringing your attention directly into this moment. Focusing your mind on an anchor will serve you well as you practice these new ways of bringing your attention into the present, and keeping your mental and emotional responses balanced and easy.

The amount of stress you can create for yourself by being swept up in thoughts and feelings is surprising, so being able to take the charge out of them can go a long way toward relieving it.

Things You've Learned in This Chapter

+ A more detailed exploration of the definitions and distinctions of meditation and mindfulness

+ States of mind you might confuse with mindfulness, and why they are not meditation *or* mindfulness

+ How to do walking meditation

+ What anchors are and how they work

- Recognizing the tendency to create preferences, and how they can contribute to the state of tension and stress

- Meditation on your sense of hearing

Creating the Mindfulness Habit: Week 3
Practice, Part 1

Each day, choose one or two of the activities you learned in Weeks 1 and 2 (square breathing, the three-part breath, standing meditation, sense of touch) to practice. Practice them mindfully, giving them your full attention.

Take note of how you feel before and after you do the activity. You can either set aside a specific time to do it, or, as you begin to notice your opportunities to practice more and more often, do it as part of your everyday activities if you remember or decide to. Be sure to keep notes on your experiences in your journal. Again, the journal is a tool for fully considering and spending time with your experiences and will assist you in integrating them into your mind and body more fully and more deeply.

Practice, Part 2

Practice the meditation on listening each day. Again, you can make this something for which you create a time to practice, and if the opportunity arises, you could choose to do it as part of your everyday activities. It can be just a few moments, or set your timer and go for ten minutes. Vary the kind of place that you practice it.

If you would like, one time this week you may choose a piece of music to listen to for your mindful listening. Choose something instrumental (no vocal, no lyrics), and it is better to find something unfamiliar. Listen to this as you would any other sounds, letting the music unfold and reveal itself to you. This version can be both easier and more difficult than listening to the random sounds that you experience in a room or outside, as music can have an intellectual and emotional component. If the music provokes feelings for you, you don't have to pretend not to have them; just acknowledge that they are occurring and don't fall down the rabbit hole into them. Observe and accept them as you would any thoughts or feelings, and then come back to the present moment. Integrate your sense of touch with this experience if you find it very difficult to let go of an emotional charge.

Make notes in your journal about when you decided to practice listening, what you felt like before you began and what you felt like after you finished. These descriptions are for your purposes only, so use whatever kind of descriptive language you choose that best expresses your experiences, sensations, and feelings.

Practice, Part 3

Practice walking meditation at least three times this week. Each time, make notes in your journal. Consider the following questions in relationship to your experiences:

1. When did you choose to do the walking meditation?

2. What did you notice in your body while you were walking? What did you notice in your mind?

3. What caused you to struggle and what did you find rewarding?

4. What did you notice at the end?

5. As you practiced it over time, what changed for you?

6. Now that you've done it a couple of times, what ways could you see to integrate this into your life?

Habit Building

Continue to keep an awareness open to times and places where it would be possible for you to use the techniques you've learned so far. Again, it is okay if you still think of them or notice them after the fact, even hours later, but now you will begin to also notice them in time.

Be sure to use your journaling pages to make notes recording when opportunities arise, including (or especially!) the ones you find yourself taking advantage of. If you have, be sure to make note of any changes in your body or mind that you notice after doing them.

———

You are now halfway through the program. Change comes gradually, and gradual change can be hard to notice. Keeping notes on your experiences will, along with promoting habit formation, give you an important place to reflect on your experiences, integrating them more fully. In addition, you will have something to reference and reflect back on so you can track your change better.

You're doing GREAT. Keep doing your best. I am rooting for you because I know that you can do this, and I am so excited for you as you make new discoveries.

Namaste.

CHAPTER 4

Week 4

Short-Term Goals, Long-Term Benefits

The end result of learning this material can, of course, include a greater ability to be present, as well as an improved sense of relaxation, and a decrease in the amount of anxiety, worry, and anger. But it might be interesting for you to know that further down the line, those benefits then provide even more rewards.

Being more mindful and having a spacious mind can bring you improved body awareness. This gives you a window into your wellness and other benefits such as increased coordination. Being more in touch with your body provides you with a valuable tool for gauging your emotional state and reactivity, allowing you to be present with those feelings.

That quiet mind also sets the stage for gentle but profound personal insights and understanding as you let go of the noise and chaos that have been affecting you inside and out. The ability to be mindful and present has also been linked to increased levels of compassionate thought and action as you have the space and clarity to really see others.

Letting Go of Intention

We've reached the fourth week, and right about now you are probably starting to feel some anticipation. It is normal that you would be starting to anticipate seeing the big payoff for your efforts. If you've been practicing and doing your journaling, you are seeing some marked changes. Even if you've not been as committed to it as perhaps you would have liked, it is likely that you've noticed some benefits. But maybe not—maybe they're not very apparent to you yet. Changes that are slow and gradual can often only be seen in retrospect.

Are you wondering if this is really going to have the life-changing effects that I have been dangling in front of you? Are you wondering if this is really going to meet your expectations for what you thought would happen?

Consciously or unconsciously, you came into this process with expectations for how it would unfold, what the benefits would look like, feel like, and how quickly you would see progress. I am now going to ask you to go against your instincts, to let go of all your assumptions and expectations, and surrender to the process.

Here's a story one of my teachers told me. During a talk at the Zen center where I practice, a student said to the head teacher, "Doing *zazen* [sitting meditation] has really helped me with my anger. When I am feeling really angry, I do *zazen*, and I feel myself calm down and the anger goes away."

The teacher responded by grumbling, "*Please* don't use *zazen* for that."

"Okay," you are saying, "what am I supposed to learn from *that* story? That sounds pretty discouraging to me." The teacher's answer might come across as confusing or contradictory. It may strike you as counterintuitive. After all, you came here because you were looking for support, for a resolution of a problem, for results. You want to be relieved of your anxiety, stress, worry—and yes, even anger. Why would a teacher discourage his student from sitting with the intention of relieving his anger?

There are a couple different layers to examine here. The first one is the nature of meditation and mindfulness practice itself. These activities are not well suited for goal setting. Keeping a goal in mind while trying to bring yourself back to the present moment is wanting to see a sky full of stars during the daytime. You can work at it all you want. You'll be spending a lot of energy and time, but you'll not accomplish much. With mindfulness, things come in their own time, when the conditions are ripe.

Goals are about being in the future, not the present. Focusing on goals takes your attention out of the present and into an imaginary future that doesn't yet exist. The prize is found right in front of you, here and now.

So let's look at the idea of setting goals. Maybe you are wondering, what's wrong with having a goal? You've been told over and over in a hundred different ways about manifestation and the benefits of visualizing your ultimate outcome. So why would this be any different?

The distinction is that goals can have different levels of specificity and detail. It's about long-term goals versus short-term intentions.

Short-term intentions are about the immediate, not the big picture. They are about the specific, not the general. Short-term intentions focus on satisfying your specific, immediate needs, likely ignoring, and potentially sacrificing, those things that will help you achieve long-term success. You *should* feel empowered to think about, visualize, or set a goal toward being happier, less anxious, more peaceful and free. But when you create a mental checklist of expectations or artificial benchmarks of success, you get distracted by a game of "Are we there yet?"

Focusing on a particular goal or outcome can cause your mind to become so busy looking for evidence of progress toward that goal, that it's never quite allowed to get quiet. It's always striving, craving, searching.

Keep your attention on that general, long-term goal in the back of your mind. In the meantime, the short-term goals that you believe you need to meet may not be the ones that turn out to serve your long-term needs best. We sometimes are blind to our larger needs, and by putting your attention on what you might think is your ideal goal, you may be missing the other opportunities for insight and growth that arise. Allow yourself to be surprised by the experiences you have. The things you *need* to know will reveal themselves if you let them.

Don't let me discourage you: having a goal can be helpful. One of the most important things it can provide you is motivation. Knowing there is a light at the end of the tunnel, a pot of gold at the end of the rainbow, and dessert at the end of dinner, can be just the thing to keep you on track.

However, deciding that the light will be neon, the pot of gold will be rings, or that dessert will be cheesecake can not only get you off track, it can be a source of disappointment. No matter how pretty the jewelry or yummy the dessert, if you've gotten yourself into a place where you are eagerly anticipating cheesecake and someone gives you peach pie, you are going to be just a bit disappointed.

I am not saying that you shouldn't set goals. I am saying that when you do so, it should be done with the same sort of quiet, mindful attention that you are trying to bring to the other things you are doing, and to do so with an open mind and heart.

One of my teachers talks about "dim vision, big vow." If you don't intuitively grasp the meaning of this phrase right away, let me give you a bit of explanation. Think of it like this: look forward with an eye on the horizon, allowing yourself to be flexible in how you end up getting there, but move forward with deep commitment and energy. The journey *is* the destination, so experience it all, moment by moment.

Trust in the process. I can tell you from experience that if you put in the effort and attention, one day you'll suddenly realize that your reactivity and anxiety are not there—at least, not the way that they were. It sneaks up on you, in a good way!

As you go through these exercises and lessons, week by week, just do them with an open mind and heart. Do them with optimism, but try to do them without concern for how well you're doing or trying to measure some kind of progress. Let go of intention, and enter into the present moment of each exercise. *That* is where the calm and peace can be found that will displace your worry, anxiety, and distraction.

Making It Hard, Making It Easier

One of the things I want to stress to you as you learn these new skills for thinking and living is that it should be something that you don't mind doing. It should feel pretty simple, and it should feel that way because it *is* simple. If you see it as simple, you will do it. If you find it pleasant, you'll do it. If you get away from the "no pain, no gain" mentality, you will do it.

This should feel good. It should not be too hard. You are not asking yourself to do anything that you are not ready and able to do, so why not surrender to the goodness? You will get a lot better results than you will by fighting it. I can't tell you how much of my time as a teacher I spend trying to convince people to let go and surrender. In my experience, letting yourself flow into and trust the structure to support you can be very rewarding.

I know for a fact that the more you practice this material, the more interesting and rewarding you will find it. The more you experience the benefits of practicing, the more likely you are to initiate the "crave" aspect of habit formation, and this reinforces the habit of being mindful.

This sounds like a good thing, doesn't it? So why might you want to make it hard? There is a story that many people have in their minds that anything that is worthwhile and produces results can only be achieved by great and strenuous effort.

Great effort is a wonderful thing, but being too invested in the idea that you have to sweat your way to success may have been part of what led you here to begin with. You may have been certain that in order to create a space for peace and a quiet, focused mind, you had to enter into a rigid, time-consuming discipline, and expend an enormous amount of time and energy. Now you are here, and I am going to help you get past that.

If you are convinced that it *must* be hard, despite my telling you otherwise, you may find yourself trying—even if it means going out of your way to do so—to make it hard. This sounds crazy, but I see people doing it all the time. There are times I've done it myself.

Here's a guideline: If it feels too hard, you may want to begin by asking yourself gently, "Is it possible that I am making it harder than it needs to be?" You don't have to analyze why or how you are doing this; often just asking the question is enough to shift things. So let's ask some more questions.

There is a saying: "Sunlight is the best antiseptic." Just the act of bringing things out where you can see them is often enough to cause them to be resolved! Getting the stuff out that keeps you from moving forward now will make the next half of your six weeks unfold more smoothly and productively.

⧗ Exercise 4-1: Getting Clear on Your Blocks

Let's take a look at the ways you might be keeping things from flowing as freely as possible. This series of questions is a way of supporting you in recognizing your own patterns of thought and behavior. There is no value judgment on my part in how I've posed them, and no one will know how you answer but you, so I ask that you respond from the heart, and put no judgment on your answers for yourself either.

Before you go through this section, stop for a minute and do one of the exercises you've learned so far to quiet your mind. Then just address each one individually, letting the answer arise on its own, with as much clarity as you have, and then move on.

On a scale of one to five, with one being "that's certainly not me" and five being "you're reading my mind," respond to the following statements:

1. I am kind of a perfectionist. I like it when I am good at something right away, and I am a bit unforgiving with myself when I am not.

2. I believe that there is nothing to be gained that does not involve some discomfort. Success requires struggle and great effort.

3. What we've been doing in this course makes me feel things I am uncomfortable feeling.

4. Some of these exercises don't fit well into my skill set. I often feel overwhelmed or inadequate to the task.

Which question did you score the highest number on?

Which question did you score the second highest number on?

Now that you have some insight into patterns of resistance you may have, they are much more likely to be resolved. In the next section, you can look at some ways to address your blocks and make things go a little easier for yourself.

Some Ways to Rethink Your Blocks

Here are some new ways to look at your patterns of resistance and begin to develop more balance. From the list above, find the number that corresponds with your biggest challenge. Read the list of ideas for that number below, and put a check mark next to the one(s) that you think will be helpful to you. Then do the same with any other challenges you may have.

1. *Are you a perfectionist?*

    + If you knew how to do this, if you were really skilled at it, you'd have done it by now. Give yourself permission to not be very good at it. Doing this is not settling; it is showing yourself the patience and compassion you would offer someone else.

    + Hold the knowledge in your heart that eventually, and without warning, you will get better at it.

    + Have faith that what you are doing right now is beneficial and worthwhile. Don't compare yourself to where you think you should be.

    + Consider what you are measuring yourself against. Is the scale real? Is it fair?

2. *Do you subscribe to the belief in "no pain, no gain"?*

    + Give yourself permission to enjoy the journey without focusing on the reward. The reward is happening—it's just very, very subtle.

- This really is hard work, even if you don't recognize it.

- Are you so convinced that this must be hard that you are looking for trouble? Are you thinking you must be missing something? Quietly and gently ask yourself if it is possible that you are making it harder than it needs to be.

3. *Does this course make you feel things you are uncomfortable feeling?*

- This can be part of the process. You are opening up to being present with yourself. This is a very good thing. These feelings, like all things, are temporary and can be addressed with calm and self-nurturing attention, and without indulgence or drama.

- With each exercise, you have a choice to do it or not do it. Different periods of time in your life are conducive to different kinds of experiences, so something that seems way too hard right now may be just what you need next month, next week, or tomorrow. Skip that particular exercise for now, but consider returning to it soon. There is probably a rich vein of material in there for you, or as one of my teachers used to say, "There's cheese down that hole."

+ Avoiding those feelings will not make them disappear,
  but you can only handle what you can right now.
  There is strong sensation and there is pain. Hanging
  in there can provide you with a wonderful surprise
  regarding your own strength and resiliency. Make a
  conscious choice to stop or move forward, and then
  be okay with your decision.

4. *Do you feel like the exercises don't fit into your skill set?*
   Like you just can't do them?

   + Go ahead and continue with the activities, but be gentle
     with yourself, and meet yourself where you are, right
     now. Do the best you can and accept that it is enough.

   + Not every exercise you learn here is right for
     everyone at every time. Some things might come
     more naturally than others. If after you give
     something a fair shot and examine the
     possibilities it just feels wrong, then move on.

Relax. Be kind to yourself. You'll get it.

Remember, if you are thinking ...	Then you should know ...
Anything that is worthwhile and produces results can only be achieved by strenuous effort.	Great effort is a wonderful thing, but it is not the same thing as strenuous effort. You already have enough things in your life that are hard. I'm making the road smooth for you; commit to enjoying it.
Anything good for me must be somewhat unpleasant.	This isn't cod liver oil. Do you love a fresh, ripe peach? A walk through the leaves on a crisp, autumn day? A massage? Why do you think they make gummy vitamins?
"No pain, no gain."	Let go of it; it will not serve you here. Healthy habits become habits because they feel good. Didn't you come here because you want your life to flow? To feel smooth, calm, and easy? Remember, getting there is half the fun.

The Senses: Tasting

You've spent some time with the senses of touch and hearing so far, and found out what it is like to enter the moment by using one of these as an anchor at any number of different times and places. Now we'll look at the sense of taste. Taste can be useful as a meditative moment that you can use anytime you eat, drink, or pop a breath mint.

The sense of taste is a richly layered experience. It is made even richer because using your sense of taste also relies, to some extent, on the senses of touch and smell. The texture of food in your mouth is an integral part of eating, along with the sense of smell, but you generally cluster it together as one experience.

This activity creates a bridge from being present with a single, simple experience to more complex activities.

It is also an experience that many of the people I have shared it with find to be quite profound. I have had people practice this activity with food they actively dislike, only to discover that the layers of experience change their relationship (even if only partially) to that food.

It is fun to eat a meal this way, but it takes quite a bit of time and concentration, so unless you're living in a hermitage, this is not a great way to experience all your meals. It is something that you can add as a part of any meal, however. Even your cup of afternoon tea or coffee can be an opportunity for a blissful return to the present moment.

To get the fullest experience, you should begin practicing this mindfulness exercise with eating food, but you can make it flexible, to fit many occasions, by doing it with a delicious cup of coffee, fresh juice, or a glass of wine. Whenever it feels right.

As in previous exercises, read through the instructions once before practicing this exercise.

⏳ Exercise 4-2: The Mindful Meal

Prepare your eating space with everything you will need: serving and eating utensils, condiments, napkin, etc. Remove unnecessary distractions such as the radio or television.

Take a moment to bring your attention on to your food. Take a portion of your food and put it in your mouth, but *do not start chewing*. Let the food sit in your mouth and notice its temperature, its weight on your tongue, and any tastes or sensations that begin to reveal themselves.

With all your attention, bite down into the food in your mouth. Feel the resistance against your teeth, and be aware if there is a burst of texture or flavor. Slowly chew your bite, allowing the flavors to wander about your mouth, allowing yourself to be surprised by unsuspected layers of flavor and texture.

Identifying words may come to mind such as salty, juicy, or sweet, but do not look for labels. Just allow the flavors to exist as an experience.

When your food is chewed thoroughly, mindfully swallow, feeling your tongue send the food down to nourish your body.

Take a second bite of food, keeping your mind open to the experience being new and different from the first one. Continue eating this way as long as it pleases you to do so.

It's time to record your experience in your journal by answering the following questions.

Questions for Exercise 4-2

1. What five words (more or less) would you use to describe your experience with your food? How was it different from how you've experienced eating in the past?

2. What surprised you about this experience?

3. What did you gain from this technique?

4. Imagine what it would be like to eat at least a little bit of everything you consume during the day this way. Does that idea appeal to you?

5. How might it change your relationship to eating?

The Mindful Walk

In the last lesson, you learned about walking meditation, and we explored the idea of mindful walking. The difference, as we defined it, is that walking meditation is walking with the strict purpose of doing it for its own sake, allowing your body and mind to become more present. It has a set of movements and behaviors that varies from the walking you do naturally during the day.

On the other hand, walking mindfully is more about bringing a different kind of awareness to a more everyday activity, with the addition of an increased attention to your actions and your surroundings. It might seem like this is a simpler task than the walking meditation, but it is actually more complex. It seems simpler because there is less structure and fewer proscribed details to pay attention to. But that's exactly what makes it more difficult. When you have a few very specific things to pay attention to, and most of them are not occurring at the same time, you can really put all of your attention on those few things, or on one thing. When you've been given a large pool of sensory input to work within, it becomes more challenging.

The narrow focus of foot leaving the ground, foot moving through the air, foot touching the ground, is concrete and specific. There is no need for you to pick and choose, and picking and choosing—and then committing to that choice—is much harder.

You've practiced using your senses individually so far—touching, listening, and tasting—as an anchor for your attention. You've practiced resting your attention on the movement of your body through space and in relationship to itself. What happens when you bring it all together?

It's time to go for a mindful walk.

There are a few different ways that you can approach the mindful walk. It is best that you decide before you begin which one you are going to do this particular time. Changing your mind constantly will not provide you with the opportunity to go as deep into the experience as you might and will make it far less rewarding.

Limiting your choices can set you up for success. Having too many choices can cause your mind to spin out, as suddenly you find yourself considering, weighing, deciding, changing your mind, and then questioning those choices. Too many choices can be an important cause of stress. It may seem the opposite of what you'd think, but having limitations provides a structure that is very supportive and allows you to stop juggling your thoughts and bring your attention more fully into what you are doing.

How do you choose which approach is right for you? Just go with your gut instinct; choose whatever sounds good, or, if you're in that kind of mood, try the one that sounds the most challenging. If it turns out you wish you'd tried a different one, try that one next time. Remember, what's right (or wrong) now can exactly fit your state of mind and circumstances later, so come back to the list of options each time.

⏳ Exercise 4-3: Mindful Walking

Choose one of the following approaches for taking a mindful walk. It is probably best to start with about ten to fifteen minutes of mindful walking time. This is actually quite a lot. If you want to take a longer walk, do the ten to fifteen minutes of mindful walking first, then continue to walk as you choose after that.

Variation 1

Walk using just one of your senses as a primary anchor:

+ The physical feeling of your gait as your feet hit the ground

+ The sounds that come and go as you move through your environment

+ The smells that waft over, through, and past you

Continue to bring your attention back to that sense over and over, whenever thoughts, reactions, or opinions arise. This is the least complicated, but requires an extended period of attention in one area.

Variation 2

Decide on more than one of your senses you will use on your walk, and set a recurrent timer on your phone or watch to alert you every five to ten minutes. At the timer, switch to the next sense, bringing your attention fully to that experience for that period of time.

This has more variety, but the trick is to not anticipate the switch to the next sensory anchor, only paying attention to what you are experiencing here and now.

Variation 3

Walk in a *shikantaza* style. *Shikantaza* translates as "just sitting," and it is one of the ways of practicing sitting meditation. The approach is to practice it with the idea of "just sitting"—not focusing on anything in particular, no mantra, no special breathing, no anchor. In the case of practicing your mindful walking, just walk, allowing the experiences of movement and sensory input to move over, through, and around you, noticing them as they arise and fall away.

A way of addressing having to be mindful within a large pool of sensory input options is to let it all be around you without *having* to choose, only allowing your experiences to arise and fall, just like your thoughts. This is a great way to try being present with an activity and can be very rewarding.

Think of it as if you were a fish swimming through water. As you move along, you are aware of spots in the water that are warm or cool, or places that have lots of small fish or plankton that sweep past as you move through it. For some people, this is the most difficult to do properly as it requires you to really quiet your mind without the support of a specific anchor; others find it simplest of all.

Questions for Exercise 4-3

1. Which type of mindful walk did you choose to do? Why did you choose it?

2. What did you find was most difficult during your mindful walk?

3. Were you able to continue bringing your attention back to your anchor?

4. What did you discover from your walk? About yourself? About the environment?

5. When can you imagine using this in your activities?

Chapter 4 Summary

When you find yourself becoming involved in analyzing your expectations and intentions, you are cheating yourself out of the opportunity of watching the present unfold for itself. Learning to surrender is a powerful ability. It leads to being able to stay in the moment, even when things go sideways.

Being able to relax into the unfolding of your new experiences and allow them to be pleasant is a profound gift to yourself, and a stress-buster of its own. Taking the time to see what makes things hard can lift some burdens off of your shoulders.

You have so many resources in your body for bringing you into the present and rooting your attention in the moment: your muscles, your organs, your senses. The important thing is to choose one and commit to it with completeness and consistency, constantly bringing your attention back to the present moment with patience and kindness to yourself.

Things You've Learned in This Chapter

+ How expectation and intention can be blocks

+ The importance of "dim vision, big vow"

+ What your personal blocks may be to entering into this process with joy

+ Some resolutions to your blocks

+ What mindful eating is and how to do it

+ How mindful walking takes mindfulness out into the world

Creating the Mindfulness Habit: Week 4
Practice, Part 1

Each day, choose any one of the activities you learned in the first three weeks to practice. Practice it mindfully, giving it your full attention. Take notes on how you feel before and after you do it. You can either set aside a specific time to do it, or do it as part of your everyday activities as you remember.

Practice, Part 2

Two more times this week (total of three), take a fifteen-minute mindful walk. You may always use the same approach, or you can try all of them in turn. Afterward, make notes on your experiences in your journal. Use the following questions as a starting point:

- When did you decide to walk? Why that time or day?

- Which approaches did you try?

- Did you like one of them better? If so, which one and why?

- How did it feel different from taking a regular walk?

Practice, Part 3

Enjoy a meal or part of a meal mindfully two times this week, and one beverage, hot or cold. Take the time to write about your experiences in your journal beginning with the following questions:

- What meal have you chosen, and why you have chosen it?

- How were each of these experiences similar to each other? How were they different from each other?

- How were they the same or different from the first time you tried mindful eating?

Habit Building

Continue to keep an awareness open to times and places that are well suited to using the techniques you have learned so far. Notice which activities seem appropriate. Also make note of any favorites or fallbacks.

If you've been primarily focused on doing only one particular mindfulness activity—for example, breathing—choose another to try.

Continue to use your journaling pages to make notes recording when opportunities arise, including the ones you find yourself taking advantage of. Be sure to make note of any changes in your body or mind that you notice after doing them.

———

If you've been giving this project some effort, you are probably beginning to notice some things. Some of those things might be a surprise. Some of them might be revelations. Some might be a bit uncomfortable. Hang in there. We'll deal with uncomfortable soon. In the meantime…

Namaste.

CHAPTER 5

Week 5

We're coming in on the homestretch of this journey as you start the second to last lesson of cultivating the Mindfulness Habit.

Congratulations on your commitment to taking charge of your well-being, dedicating your time and energy to living a better life. You have already seen the rewards and benefits that come from developing the habit of finding ways to be mindful. What you haven't yet seen are the long-term benefits. Exactly what in your life will be better, happier, more peaceful, more clear will depend on who you are and where you started. But now that you've begun to develop the Mindfulness Habit, when you look back six, nine, twelve months from now, you'll be delighted by how much you've changed.

Opening Up Time and Space

I hope that you have been enjoying using the senses of hearing and touch as a way to bring yourself into the present moment. You may now be noticing a sense of spaciousness that settles into those moments of mindful presence. That spaciousness may feel very calming. It may feel like your mind has a chance to get quiet, and like time slows down or gets stretched out.

This change in how you are perceiving time is wonderful. It allows each moment to be rich and full of opportunity for wonder. Experiencing five or ten minutes every once in a while of coming to the realization and recognition of time as a function of perception and the mind can really put a different spin on things.

When I was nineteen years old, I was on a scaffold twenty-five feet in the air when it tipped over. In my perception, the time it took from the moment when I realized I was going over until I hit the ground felt like about twenty or thirty minutes. Of course it was only a few seconds, but it seemed like so much happened in that time. There are many things that can cause changes in time perception, and the kind of trauma that I experienced in that moment is one of them. When that fall happened to me, my attention became incredibly focused on every millisecond and what I was experiencing in it.

When you let your mind become quiet and in the present, the imposed structure of time drops away. You can experience each segment of each moment more fully and completely, and each one stands out, distinct and clear. This creates that feeling of spaciousness and stretched time. It is very refreshing and lovely.

Now, if this has not happened to you, do not become disappointed or think you've made a mistake. It will happen when it happens, in the way that it makes sense for it to happen to you. But it's not a goal to pursue or an experience to crave. It's just something to notice, just like any other experience.

This feeling of open space and time leads your mind from being in a reactive state to being in a more receptive state, one in which you can be in the middle of circumstances without being overwhelmed by them. This is where you begin to develop a state of equanimity.

Equanimity: The Middle Path

Equanimity is a state of being that is balanced, clear minded, and dispassionate. It's about accepting things as being the way they are. Equanimity is a state of calm acceptance of the present set of circumstances. It's knowing how to be accepting of the things that you don't have any control over, at least for the moment. Equanimity can seem a lot like apathy. In fact, apathy is sometimes called the "near enemy" of equanimity. They can be very close, but one can sneak in, pretending to be the other, and wreak havoc. If you are wondering what the difference is between apathy and equanimity, a simple way to look at it is: apathy is "I don't care," and equanimity is "I'm okay." Apathy is a decision not to take action; equanimity is accepting that there may be no action to take—at least, none that will constructively change the present circumstances. Equanimity may also allow you to see that there are options for action, but to come at them from a balanced point of view, without a lot of baggage, drama, or bias.

Equanimity has the wonderful characteristic of providing you with the opportunity to see and embrace the temporary state of things. As you see that the present circumstances are only as they exist at that specific time and place, you find that you no longer need to be concerned for or invested in the future outcome or condition, nor slip back into being preoccupied with things that happened in the past.

This ability to see and acknowledge the temporary state of affairs also helps create equanimity. As you see that each thing that is happening is part of only this one moment, and that you only have to be in this one moment, and not concern yourself with the next, you can maintain a sense of balance and peace around even the most trying of events.

It is important to maintain equanimity not only when things are difficult, stressful, painful, or hopeless, but also when your mood is high, when you are optimistic and filled with jubilance and joy. These too are temporary and not only can you be taken out of being present and mindful by these feelings of great joy, but when they finally come to an end, the crash can be very unpleasant.

It can set you up for some unhealthy behaviors that will cause you to create events and attitudes that cause mood swings just to keep the rush going.

As you might imagine, this pattern of thought and behavior is not healthy for your body or your mind.

Remember what you read earlier in this book about how being mindful helps bring you into the present state and helps remove the need for worrying about the past or anticipating the future? Now that you have learned more about how to be in the present, equanimity is what helps you find a state of balance and remain there. Developing an understanding for what that sense of balance feels like can help you break the pattern of creating a lot of emotional drama and produce a greater sense of contentment that is less exciting, but a lot less exhausting and stressful.

In this lesson, you'll be exploring more ways of making use of your senses, and then bringing all your senses back to a deeper exploration of mindful daily activity. This is where you make the leap into mindfulness being more fully integrated into your everyday life.

Mindful Activity

In the last chapter, you learned about walking mindfully. Now we move into the realm of other mindful action. Think back to the walking meditation you learned in Chapter 3. Remember how you put your attention on each part of the walking experience, feeling your body move, your weight shift, and the sensation of your feet making and breaking contact with the floor? This is a good reminder for the kind of attention-paying that you will want to bring into opportunities to be mindful in your everyday life, at home, at work, at play.

You have already begun to experience how paying close attention to your actions can begin to bring your mind to a quiet point of focus. You may have also noticed that when it happens, your body begins to let go of some of the symptoms of stress. As a result, you may feel healthier, calmer, or more clear.

Turning a simple task into a chance to be completely present has several benefits. You find that you will be more efficient and careful in what you do as you bring more of yourself to whatever activity you engage in. Being more present will make you better at what you are doing and bring greater attention and focus. When you bring your full attention to any task, you perform it more accurately and thoroughly.

Tasks you thought of as boring can become deeply fascinating. It is an opportunity to shift your relationship to what you are doing, changing how you look upon and approach the tasks you have always found tiresome or repetitive.

Things that you found stress-inducing can become profoundly relaxing. You will begin to find simple pleasure in many of the things you take for granted every day.

Finally, it allows you an endless supply of opportunities to focus and quiet your mind. *Everything you do* is now an opportunity to create an instant point of focus, bringing you back to the here and now, quieting the anxious, angry, or distracted mind.

Every day, throughout the day, you are doing things. You are walking to the bus stop, emptying the dishwasher, making coffee, shopping for groceries, cleaning the bathroom sink, sorting, stacking, prioritizing, making phone calls…you get the idea.

Most of these things you are doing—heck, almost all of them—can be turned into anchors for focusing and quieting the mind.

I will have you start off simply with the following activity and you'll see what I mean. I am very excited for you to try this, because I think you will enjoy it, and it can really begin to open up your options for opportunities to be more present.

Exercise 5-1: Mindful Activity

This exercise is very simple. It's taking something you take for granted and turning it into an opportunity. Let's start off with a list of things that most of us do regularly. I want you to start with something relatively uncomplicated. There will be plenty there to keep you challenged and interested.

Pick one of the following activities to perform. These activities are intentionally very simple; don't complicate things by adding to them.

+ Wash your hands

+ Brush your teeth

+ Fold laundry

+ Put away clean dishes

Before you begin, take a very brief moment to gather your attention. Doing something like a couple of mindful breaths or the standing meditation can be helpful to get your head in the right place.

As you begin your activity, remember your experience with working with your senses of touch, taste, and hearing. Give your attention to each motion, experiencing it fully and completely. Resist the urge to analyze or critique your experience.

Let each segment of your process stand as a separate event that you can allow yourself to enter into fully. In one moment you may be experiencing things predominantly with your sense of touch, in the next with your sense of sight or smell, or with a combination of more than one. Whatever you are experiencing, do so fully.

If you begin to find yourself drifting into the realm of thought or memory, only notice that this has happened, and then bring your attention back to your toothbrush, your dishes, or your laundry basket, and let your attention rest on the experience of that moment.

If it turns out to be harder than it looks, that's okay—it certainly can be. But also give yourself permission for it to be more enjoyable than it looks, too. I think you are likely to be pleasantly surprised.

Now write in your journal about your experience. Use the following questions as inspiration for your writing.

Questions for Exercise 5-1

1. What activity did you choose?

2. What was challenging about doing your task mindfully? What were the stumbling blocks?

3. What were the rewards of doing your task mindfully? What were the surprises?

4. How did the way you felt before doing your task compare to the way you felt after doing your task?

Exercise 5-2: More Complex Mindful Activity

Now that you've tried doing a simple activity mindfully, I am going to challenge you to do a more complete and complex one. Before you begin, keep the following things in mind:

+ This can take a lot of effort. Don't bite off more than you can chew.

+ You *will* find yourself slipping out of being present and into thinking, analyzing, pondering, and remembering. Just keep bringing your attention back to your immediate experience.

+ Maintain a balance between appreciating the colors, textures, sounds, and scents, and getting caught up in them. If your appreciation comes in and then moves through, it is likely you are staying in the present. If you find yourself sinking into one of your sensory responses to the exclusion of others, or if it builds on itself and becomes all consuming, then you have left the present moment.

+ If you find yourself straying out of the moment, stop and bring your attention back to your breath, or do a standing meditation for a moment before returning to the activity.

Ready to begin? Pick one of the following activities to do. This will be your mindful activity.

+ Shower or bathe

+ Dress yourself head to toe

- Blow-dry your hair

- Sort, wash, and dry a load of laundry

- Shovel snow, vacuum, or sweep the floor

- Wash your car

- Wash dishes

Before you start, take a very brief moment to gather your attention, focus your thoughts, and quiet your body.

Be sure to give your attention to each motion, experiencing it fully and completely. Resist the urge to analyze or critique your experience. Allow yourself to sink into the richness of the experience, but not to the exclusion of your overall awareness. In other words, don't follow some pleasant sensory aspect of the experience down a rabbit hole.

Notice how each part of your activity is its own separate moment, perfect and distinct, how it arises and then drifts away as the next one arises.

You may notice your sense of time changing, expanding and contracting. If you do notice this, be sure not to get caught by it; avoid letting your curiosity or your fascination take your attention there instead of keeping it on your task, which, in this case, is where it belongs.

When you find you've lost track, gotten lost in thinking about something, or drifted off, choose one aspect of your experience such as texture, or color, or your breathing as a touchstone to bring you gently back into relationship with your activity.

When you have finished, take a moment to notice how you feel. Think about how you felt before you began and also how you felt while you were doing your mindful activity and what you noticed. Remember to make notes in your journal to help solidify your experience.

Chapter 5 Summary

When you start to open up to all the things that are available to your experience in each and every moment, you can see how much is there, and also see how much space there is in between. It's like the photographs that are taken through microscopes—photomicrographs—that show all the space that exists inside the things we perceive as solid. Taking a moment to stop and go into your experiences with concentration opens all that space up with your mind as well.

This sense of time opening up and the spaciousness that is created can be very soothing. Suddenly, it doesn't feel as though everything is happening at once, but that there is only the thing that is happening now, and there is quite a lot of time for it to happen.

The spacious mind, the quiet mind, creates fertile ground for the cultivation of equanimity, a state of healthy balance and resilience of the mind. It is like a keel on a boat, the fin that extends down into the water, that keeps the boat from listing too far to one side or the other. It allows the boat to tilt but helps prevent it from going so far that it turns over.

You're now getting a chance to take the skills in mindfulness that you've been developing and bring them to activities that are part of your everyday life. This is where, as they say, the rubber meets the road. You have the skills and awareness you need in order to go forward and be mindful a million times a day if you want to—and why wouldn't you?

You've spent quite a while developing this sense of what it means to be mindful, so now it is time to challenge yourself, step forward, and reap the rewards.

Things You've Learned in This Chapter

+ How quieting the mind opens up a sense of spaciousness that is calming and provides clarity

+ How within that spaciousness, your perception of time changes

+ What equanimity is, and why it's a good thing

+ How a quiet, spacious mind is fertile ground for developing equanimity

+ The benefits of practicing the mindful execution of small tasks

- How to bring the mindfulness skills you have been developing into your everyday activities

Creating the Mindfulness Habit: Week 5
Practice, Part 1

Every day this week, choose one of the exercises from the first four chapters to practice. You can choose the same one each time, allowing yourself to explore and sink deeper into the experience, or you can experiment with different exercises to reflect your needs, your mood, or your circumstances. Each time, be sure to take notes in your journal. Make notes on what you chose, why you chose it, what you were experiencing in your mind and body before you began, anything interesting that happened while you were practicing, and how you felt afterward.

Practice, Part 2

Every day this week, choose a task to perform mindfully. You can decide that you want to, for example, brush your teeth mindfully every day and see what happens when you do that repeatedly over time. Or if you'd prefer, switch it up, choosing a task that you might find interesting to explore in this way. You might want to choose a task that you find particularly unpleasant or boring and see how your relationship to that task shifts when you take it on as an opportunity to be fully present. On the other hand, you may want to choose something you already take some pleasure in and then add an attentive, quiet mind to its execution and see what happens.

Use your journal to make notes on your experience. Before you begin, think about what your expectations are and then reflect back on those expectations afterward. How did your expectations and your experience match up? What surprised you?

Habit Building

As many times as possible this week, try to connect your opportunities for being more mindful and present with the information you have learned about the ways you know to make that happen.

Continue to use your journaling pages to make notes recording these match-ups. Be sure to take note of any changes in your body or mind that you notice after doing them.

These opportunities should now begin to include opportunities for you to do tasks mindfully. Be sure to make note of them in your journal pages. At this point you can be using your journal to reflect on your experiences as you find it useful, but don't abandon it yet; it's still assisting you in reinforcing your experiences, and we have a couple of weeks left to solidify your habit, so keep using your journal as a way to clarify or strengthen your relationship to what you are experiencing.

I wish I could be there with you while you are experiencing the things that are resulting from your new way of interacting with the world. If it has lifted a bit of your anxiety, your anger, or your distraction, then I am delighted, because I know that if you've begun to see that happen—even just a little bit—then it can only get better from here.

Namaste.

CHAPTER 6

Week 6

This is our last week in the structured part of this program, but it's only the beginning of your journey. In these last six weeks (or so) I hope you have witnessed some changes, some revelations, some insights, and some moments of calm. There also may have been some moments of frustration, pain, and discomfort.

This is a good thing. Really, it is. I know that previously in the book I told you that I wanted this to be easy so that you'll do it. I also know that if you have experienced painful feelings or discomfort it is because you probably *have* been doing it, because these feelings only tend to arise when you've gotten to the point where you've begun to quiet your mind enough for those things that have been stuffed in the corners to kick up a bit of a fuss.

What is happening here? When you have a lot of mental chatter, you can use it to distract yourself from having your attention to go to some things that are difficult and hard to look at. As you quiet that chatter and let your mind focus on the moment, the chatter can take on a different tone, the tone of the underlying issues you've been trying to avoid.

If this happens to you—and that's a big *if*—the thing to remember is that this is just more mental noise. It's unpleasant. It's uncomfortable. But it's just noise, and you can deal with it just like the other noise in your mind. Try acknowledging it and then bringing your attention back to your anchor—your senses, your experiences, your breathing, your walking.

Don't use the arising of unpleasant or difficult feelings or thoughts as a measure of success. They may arise or they may not; it does not have any bearing on the quality of your experience. Let your experience be your own.

Pain and the Present Moment

Mindfulness has proven to be very useful in dealing with pain—chronic pain, acute pain, and emotional pain as well. The things you have learned about acknowledging the temporary nature of each moment can serve you well.

Your quiet mind is not only an open space for emotional—and physical—pain to arise, it is also a great support in dealing with it when it does. Allowing your pain to be a part of your experience, or even the anchor for your attention, will change your experience of it. It might disperse, or it might intensify and then disperse. It might not change at all, but your perception of the discomfort can change dramatically. No matter what happens, seeing the temporary nature of the moment can be very reassuring and comforting.

It's far better to let your attention go to rest on your discomfort than to use the things you've learned as a way of avoiding it. I'm not trying to tell you that every time something uncomfortable comes up you have to dive in head first. Not every time and not every place are right for going deep into your issues, your fears, your sadness and disappointments, but it is worthwhile to take a moment to acknowledge them.

In my first encounter with allowing myself to go into discomfort, I was experimenting and the end result was eye-opening. I was a new meditator and was trying very hard to find times and opportunities to practice, especially since at the time I had a preschooler at home who was not very patient with her mommy sitting quietly, ignoring everything.

One morning I woke up early and everyone was still asleep. I lay there and thought, "Hey! Quick, go sit before somebody wakes up and it's all over." So I snuck out of the bedroom and quickly and quietly sat down. I was only settled in for a minute or two when I realized that I was thirsty. This is the kind of thirsty that you can only get from sleeping in a house in Minnesota in the winter, where our indoor air can go down to 4 percent humidity. Parched. This thirst was beyond uncomfortable; it was painful.

But I knew that the more I got up and moved around, taking a glass from the cupboard, running water, stepping on squeaking floor boards, the greater the possibility that I would lose my opportunity to the wakefulness of others, so I decided to stay seated, buck up, and see what happened. I knew that ignoring it was not going to work, that the sensations were too intense and too conspicuous for that. So since that pain was going to be front and center, I would put my attention on it. I would give it the front row seat it demanded.

Watching events unfold from this decision was one of the most fascinating things I've ever seen. At first, because of course this was something that I could have easily remedied with a simple glass of water, I had to really commit to doing this, to not just taking care of it and taking my chances that someone would wake. My innate curiosity, as much as anything, got me past that in a matter of a minute.

Then I became an observer of an amazing process. The sensations I was feeling in my throat and mouth got bigger, louder, and more intense, and as they did, they became more detailed. It became both increasingly uncomfortable and increasingly easy to tolerate. It stopped being "thirsty" and became a constellation of sensations I experienced with different parts and subparts of my body. I could watch as each sensation arose and fell away to be replaced by another. After a little while of this, the sensations began to go into greater and greater degeneration, until they seemed to dematerialize. It's not that I was no longer thirsty; it was that my relationship to the circumstances and experiences of my thirst had changed. It was just a series of small events.

Of course, when I was done sitting, I immediately got a glass of water, but by being willing to be with my discomfort and feed my curiosity about exploring my experiences, I gave myself a great gift that day.

When it comes to feeling like you are in a less-than-ideal state of health, balance, or comfort, your attention is the most powerful tool you can bring to resolving the unresolved and balancing the imbalanced. After that, your body, mind, and spirit can see and know what to do to bring you back to wellness.

Your Body as Barometer

As you have been spending more quiet time with yourself, you may have begun to notice two things. First, you may be slightly more in touch with your body, aware of its physical shape, size, and qualities, aware of when it's feeling good and not so good, along with being aware of how it responds to and reflects your emotional state.

How much you are noticing, and how this is different from the way you were experiencing it before, depends on several things:

how much you experience the world kinesthetically (through your body), how much you were aware of these things before, and what your relationship to your body has been up to this point.

There is a technique called a body scan that is a useful thing to learn. It is often taught as a long (up to 45 minutes), exhaustive trip through the body. Although I believe that this approach has its merits, for our purposes it is better to have a more abbreviated version.

Why do I think it's worthwhile for you to learn how to practice a body scan? What does it have to do with mindfulness and being in the present moment?

Way back in Week 1 we started playing with the connection between how your body relates to and reflects the things that are happening in your mental and emotional states. Spending some focused, intimate time with your body, watching how it is experiencing the world and your relationship to it, is a beautiful practice of being present—present with yourself, your environment, your experiences, and your responses.

You may have noticed there is a theme running through this book of the benefits of coming into awareness and recognition. As you bring things out of the dark corners and into the light of your attention, they begin to lose their energy, their power, and their relevance. When those things that have been causing you discomfort are allowed to come forward into your awareness, a few things can happen. Often, we are unaware of the patterns of stuck habits of the mind that we might cover up or deny. When we become more aware of their existence, these stuck patterns begin to move, move through and out, leaving you lighter and clearer. Often these feelings that we were so intimidated by, once brought out of the shadows, are recognized as being far less ominous than your memory had taught you to believe they were.

I realize that the way I am describing this process makes it sound like a series of clear, conscious decisions, but usually it's not that at all. You do not need to re-experience, conduct an analysis of, or even remember the roots and causes of your pain in order to resolve them. The human machine is a thing of great balance and functional beauty. Once it discovers the nature of a dysfunction, it moves to correct it naturally.

Letting the light of awareness shine on your pain and discomfort without an agenda, analysis, worry, or drama will initiate a shift that will remove one more unnecessary distraction from your life.

As you become more in tune with your body, you can notice many things with greater speed, insight, and clarity, and that will bring you more and more fully into the present. And in that present you will find all the things we've discovered thus far: spaciousness; a quiet, flexible, responsive mind that has great focus; a body and mind that can free itself from worry and anxiety and experience the extremes of both the great joys and great sorrows with equanimity.

⧖ Exercise 6-1: Body Scan Meditation

As always, it is important for you to read through the instructions for these exercises, but in the case of this one, it's especially important. You should probably give it more than one look before you begin, to really give yourself a sense of the flow and style of this meditation. That way if you get lost or change up the order, you can improvise effectively. If that happens, it is not a problem in any way.

You will want to set yourself up a comfortable place to practice this the first time. Find a comfortable place to lie down. Provide yourself with anything you might need in order to be comfortable. Remove all distractions, turn off the phone. If you think you will be more comfortable with a pillow for your head, or a support under your knees to protect your back, then make sure you have those handy. You may consider having a blanket available. As you become more relaxed, your metabolic rate will begin to drop and you may get chilly.

One thing I want to caution you against is that if you do this at a sleepy time of day for you, it is possible for you to get *very* sleepy and drift off. As nice as that might be, as I mentioned in an early chapter, this is not very productive, so give some consideration to when you decide to practice to best accommodate a wakeful state.

Lie on your back with your legs relaxed, maybe slightly apart, in an open, relaxed position, and your eyes open or closed, as you wish. Keeping your eyes open will help you stay awake, but closing them will assist you in going deeper into your experience.

Keep in mind that it is not necessary to understand or interpret what is going on in your body, only to pay attention as best you can. You can feel free to name things for your own reference, but don't get caught up in worrying about finding the perfect description. It is probably best to just really notice what things feel like.

Now, begin by taking a couple of deep, relaxed breaths, and then letting your breathing return to its own natural rate and depth. Bring your attention to focusing on your breathing, noticing how the air moves in and out of your body in whatever part of your body it predominates at this time and place.

See if you can get a general, global sense of yourself, both your body and mind, and how you're feeling at this particular moment. What is your quality of mind? Is it agitated, calm, curious? Don't spend a lot of time defining or analyzing, or trying to change. You're just checking in.

Check in with your body for general overall sensations of temperature pressure, stiffness, movement, stillness, weakness, or fatigue.

Now bring your attention to your chest and belly. These are areas of the body that have a distinct and immediate response to your emotional state. Check in with your chest or belly for strong sensations. Be sure not to try to change anything or figure anything out; just allow yourself to be aware of them.

Next, bring your attention down to the toes. Can you feel them without moving them? How do you become aware of your own body? How can you feel your own body? Direct your attention to your toes, imagining that you can actually breathe in through your toes, and then exhale out through them as well. Do this a couple of times, each breath bringing a light of awareness, illuminating any feelings or sensations in your toes.

Now repeat this process with your feet, breathing in awareness, letting the breath bring a clear vision of any sensations in that part of your body, being sure not to get caught up in analyzing or lost in description. It's okay if nothing really stands out, just move on to the next part of your body.

Move up to the ankles and lower legs, just allowing your attention to go to the most obvious or outer sensation at first, and then observing if more subtle or nuanced sensations arise. If a part of your body feels blank, just notice that. Notice what blank feels like.

Repeat this process with your knees and upper legs, then your buttocks and general pelvic region. As you come into the torso, you will likely notice more complex and layered sensations. Just allow yourself to experience them in whatever way they express themselves—fullness, nausea, tightness, holding, ease, movement, or lack of movement.

Continue on, moving up through your torso from belly to chest, and then to the collarbone. You can experience the torso front and back as a whole, or you can scan the spine separately depending on your preference and the amount of time you want to spend.

Breathe into your shoulders, and then into your arms and hands. Hands sometimes hold more tension and can be a greater reflection of what's going on in your body than most people think.

Now scan your neck, your throat, your face, and your head. Notice areas of tension or holding in the face and scalp.

Once more, get a general, overall impression of what your body is feeling like right now.

Now grab your journal and write about your experience. If you'd like, use the following questions as a guideline or inspiration.

Questions for Exercise 6-1

1. Did you have trouble with this technique? Did you find it enjoyable? Boring? Insight producing?

2. Did you discover anything interesting or unexpected as you allowed your attention to travel throughout your body?

3. Did you notice anything changing? Were you able to observe changes as they occurred without trying to intervene or control events?

4. Did you notice places that felt stuck or stagnant? Were you able to observe them without feeling it necessary to try to change or move them?

Variations on the Body Scan

Body scan techniques can vary widely in approach and duration and can be customized to your environment and your needs. Here are some other ways of checking in with your body. These serve different purposes, although their usefulness overlaps.

VARIATION 1

You can start this at either your head or your feet. Imagine that you have in your mind a machine that works kind of like an MRI or other scanning machine, but that it has a broad, generalized range of things that it detects—it's a "whatever is important" detector. Now imagine that this scanning beam travels up or down through your body, seeing it in slices, bringing anything interesting to your attention. Your scanner can be set to move at any speed or specificity. Notice if you begin to be invested in finding something or attaching importance to anything you find. If this happens, come back to one of your techniques, like the breath, for example, to quiet the mind. Adding intention and emotion to this technique will not provide you with as clear or true a picture as it will if you just treat it as an observation.

Allow your body to relax, ideally in a seated or reclining position, and feel it becoming heavy, connecting with the surface below it. Let your attention drift to your body, wandering around. Watch where it chooses to go and where it chooses to land. Wherever it lands, bring your attention to that place in your body without expectation or preconception, and see what you notice, what comes to your attention, its character and quality. Notice these, resisting the urge to analyze them. Just let your attention hang out in that place and watch to see what happens. If something else begins to demand your attention, allow it to drift to that spot and notice what happens there.

Sitting Meditation

It is important to me that I don't let you go without giving you an introduction to practicing a basic sitting meditation. I fully realize that not everyone is interested in taking their everyday mindfulness to this next step, but I would very much feel remiss if I didn't at least give you the opportunity to consider and try it. Even if it's not something you want to do now, it may seem appealing to you sometime in the not too distant future.

You don't have to make a commitment to doing it any particular length of time or with a particular frequency. Consider it one more tool in the box—a specialty tool that, depending on what you are interested in accomplishing, you may use often or only when it fits your requirements.

Sitting meditation is both the simplest thing and the most complex thing that I am going to teach you about. Many instructions on mindfulness and meditation jump right in with this, but I think it was worth waiting until you got to a place where you had some practice and some skills with observing the arising of thoughts and feelings and then letting them go. When you are doing sitting meditation, you are more keenly aware of this than when doing anything else you've practiced thus far, so be warned. You will need to be vigilant, but I find this to be a very rewarding practice.

This is also something that you can find an opportunity to practice in all kinds of situations. Many of the places you have found to practice the listening meditation or some of the breathing exercises might also be a good place to practice just sitting. In Japanese Zen, sitting meditation is called *zazen*, and it's the fundamental practice for bringing your mind to a profound state of quiet where the edges and differentiations between things start to minimize.

This is sometimes called "emptiness" or the void, but in fact, when your mind becomes that calm, that breakdown of barriers becomes a unique oneness with everything. This is something that people spend a long time developing, so don't expect bliss right off the bat, but you may just get a taste of it. Just remember to maintain a sense of equanimity around it, or around any other sensation, pleasant or otherwise, and not grasp at it or try to avoid it—only notice it.

⧗ Exercise 6-2: Sitting Meditation

Find a comfortable sitting position and take a moment to settle in. You can sit on a cushion on the floor or on a chair. If in a chair, be sure to be sitting upright. Do whatever you need to do so that your body feels stable, comfortable, and relatively straight. You want to find a posture that promotes wakefulness but feels easy to your body and to your mind.

It is very helpful to maintain an active upright posture and not to slouch. Setting up a good, supported posture is actually much less tiring than slouching, which can leave you uncomfortable and exhausted in a matter of minutes.

It is not a bad idea for you to set a timer for the amount of time you would like to sit. This will keep your attention from wandering to the time. It's not unreasonable to begin with as little as five minutes, but it is not hard to start with as much as fifteen.

You may choose to close your eyes while you meditate, or you might prefer to allow your eyes to softly focus on a spot several feet in front of you. Try both to see which is better for you right now. If you close your eyes, you may find it helpful when you start mentally drifting out of the moment to gently open them.

This is a very good way to bring yourself back from your musings and into the present as you get an instant visual reminder that can pull you back into your immediate surroundings.

Begin by taking several deep, relaxed breaths. Fill and empty your lungs several times, but do not strain or push. This will bring your attention to your breath, so pay attention to where you feel the breath in your body as each comes and goes.

After a few of these deep breaths, let your breathing return to its natural resting rate and depth. Bring your attention to the movement of the breath in your body and allow it to drift to where it is most obvious in your body. It may be the air moving through your nostrils, or over your upper lip; it may be in your abdomen or chest, or someplace else completely. Place your attention on that place. It is your anchor for this meditation.

Over and over, bring your attention back to the place in your body where you are experiencing your breath.

As you continue to settle in after several minutes, you may notice how the body breathes itself, how it initiates the breath effortlessly and unconsciously, and let go of any attempt to control your breathing.

Your attention will wander from your breath as thoughts begin to arise. When you realize this has happened, notice it, then bring your attention back to your anchor. You may be tempted to judge your thoughts. Notice the temptation and leave it behind, and put your attention back on the breath. It helps to just think of gently picking up your attention and gently placing it back on your anchor.

After several minutes of sitting, you may feel some frustration with the tendency of your thoughts to wander, and become irritated or judgmental toward yourself. Do not scold yourself. Be gentle with yourself, and just put your attention back on the breath. Acknowledge the movement of the mind away from the breath and then let it go as you reconnect and set your attention gently back on the anchor.

If you begin to struggle, you may want to think the words "in" and "out" as you breathe. Or you may choose to count your breaths, counting your breath until you get to five, and then starting over. These are good ways of getting back to the present. Then go back to the anchor once you feel steady and calm.

Thoughts, feelings, or sensations may continue to arise. These can be very seductive and draw your attention away from being present. You may find that you have wandered pretty far off course. It happens, so merely bring your attention back to your breath without frustration or recrimination.

Now, if you'd like to try something else, you may want to rest in the experience of the body. A good place to start is in noticing the places where the body makes contact: your seat on the chair or cushion, the place where your hands touch your knees or lap. As you open up to the body experience, notice other body sensations, but without analysis, examination, or judgment. Let go of any expectations.

When the timer goes off, gently allow yourself to be present with the space. If you'd like, place your hands together in "prayer" position and bow to close your session, expressing gratitude for the opportunity to just sit and be with the moment.

Write about your experience in your journal. You may want to use the following questions as inspiration and to help you go deeper.

Questions for Exercise 6-2

1. What was your initial overall impression of practicing sitting meditation?

2. What did you find the most difficult part of it?

3. Did you get frustrated? Were you able to let go of the frustration?

4. Did you struggle with your body at all? Did it get tired?

5. Is this something you might be interested in practicing again? What would be the best time of day to do it? Best place? Best circumstances?

Additions to Sitting Meditation

Sitting meditation can consist of working with an anchor, as you've seen, such as the breath or the body's contact with the cushion. Sometimes adding other things to your sitting can be helpful or rewarding, as can taking things away.

SHIKANTAZA: "JUST SITTING"

Some meditators try to experience *shikantaza* or "just sitting," allowing themselves to be as completely present in the moment as possible without a special technique. This may be particularly challenging to many people, but there may be times that it's just the right thing.

INTEGRATING YOUR TECHNIQUES

There is no reason that you can't use one of the primary mindfulness techniques you've learned in a formal sitting meditation. Listening, feeling the temperature of the room or the clothes on your body, or practicing the three-part breath are all things you've already done while sitting quietly.

It is important, however, that you not be a "meditation technique tourist." In other words, don't try to do everything, or even too many things, in a sitting. Choose one thing and stick with it. If you really are feeling like you've given it a good, long try, then choose something else. Meeting your resistance can be an important part of quieting your mind, and flitting from one thing to another will keep you chasing the present rather than settling into it.

As one of my yoga teachers says, "Notice how the mind gives up before the body does." Notice how quick you are to surrender to your own restlessness and sit with that.

Chanting and Mantras

Mantras and chants are another tool to focus and quiet the mind during sitting meditation. A chant or mantra is often useful when sitting with a particularly agitated mind. Some people use them at the beginning of a sit as a kind of bridge from the mental noise of daily life into a quiet mind.

If you find that doing these mantras starts to zone you out, bring you into a state of feeling "trance-y," or otherwise disconnects you from the present moment, then it is time to return to your other anchors of breath and body.

The following is a list of chants that you might consider trying. It is good to first practice them out loud. There is a particular feeling or vibration that these sounds produce in your body that you should experience. Later, you will have a sense of recall around that feeling even when practicing them silently. These ancient chants are built not only around their meaning but around the feelings the actual sounds produce.

Om (Aumm): The "universal sound." The important part of this chant is to break down the single syllable into something more like three syllables, starting with an open mouth and letting the sound be gently formed as you move your lips slowly together through an "oo" into an "mmm." Let it last as long as you can comfortably sustain it and feel the vibrations in your whole body.

So ham (so hahm or hum): "I am that." When repeated, this mantra becomes "I am that I am…" This chant is intended to be thought in your mind while following the breath. "*So*" mimics the sound of your body inhaling and is uttered in the inhale. "*Ham*" reflects the sound of the body exhaling and corresponds with the exhale. You breathe yourself into being.

Jai Ma (jay or ji mah): An expression of honoring (*jai*) Mother Earth (*Ma*), the provider of life and food.

Om shanthi, shanthi, shanthi om (aumm shontee): "Peace, peace, peace to all" (universal peace). This is very beautiful when chanted with tone and from the heart.

Gate, gate, paragate, parasamgate, bodhi svaha (gah-tay, gah-tay, para-gahtay, para-sahm-gahtay, bodee sva-ha): "Gone, gone, all gone, completely gone—awaken!" This is called the *prajnaparamita* ("perfection of wisdom") mantra and is a very sacred one for Buddhists of all traditions. It is about letting go and entering the universal oneness.

If you decide on your own chant or mantra, be sure to keep it simple and not too specific. Some people have found success using "Ave Maria" or "amen." A Hebrew or Hindu word that has great meaning for you can be a good choice, or the name of a bodhisattva or a deity, such as Avalokiteshvara, Diana, or Brahma. Be sure to let your choice resonate in your body and mind.

Chapter 6 Summary

The ability to quietly concentrate your attention that you've been gradually developing over the last several weeks has brought you to the point where you can focus your mind with a simple anchor. Although it might at first glance seem more complicated or difficult to use something that requires a lot of attention, like the walking meditation, by now you have had enough practice to perceive that the opposite is often true.

The more space you provide around your attention, the more room there is for thoughts and feelings to rush into that space, and the more effort it requires from you to keep your attention coming back to your anchor, to the present moment.

Now that you have greater use of your attention, you can turn it inward to give you some clarity and allow for insight into what your body may be reflecting about your emotional and mental states. Simply the act of tuning in to your body can be a powerful exercise. Not only is it a profound way to bring your mind to a quiet place that is completely present with your experience in your body, but connecting with those sensations in your body can cause them to shift all on their own.

This increased capacity for being able to bring your attention back to an anchor, quieting your mind, is what will allow you to now make the next step into sitting meditation. Most courses on mindfulness begin with this practice, but I believe that this is actually a place to land as a bridge to the next level. The ideas and techniques you've been working with for the last several weeks have, besides being infinitely useful on their own, developed your capacity for focus. You can bring that attention to a very concentrated way of practicing being present.

Things You've Learned in This Chapter

+ A mindful approach to physical and emotional pain

+ How your body can act as a barometer

+ How to do a body scan meditation

+ An introduction to sitting meditation

+ Things you can integrate with sitting meditation

+ Mantras

Creating the Mindfulness Habit: Week 6
Practice, Part 1

Practice the body scan at least two times this week. Try to do them at different times of the day. Pay particular attention to the difference between the two experiences, and make notes in your journal about what you notice each time and how each experience differs from the other.

Practice, Part 2

If you'd like, try some sitting meditation. Set a timer. If you sit longer than five minutes, realize that can be a long time the first time you try it. Be sure to be patient with yourself. Remember this is something that people spend a lifetime practicing.

If you decide that now is a time you'd like to give sitting meditation a try, I would recommend you try practicing it at least three times this week to get a sense for it. Sitting meditation is never the same twice. Sitting alone with your own presence with only your breath for an anchor can be wildly different from one time to the next.

Make notes in your journal each time you practice, reflecting back on your experience, but don't overanalyze or dissect that experience.

Habit Building

By now, you should be noticing that you have many, many opportunities to use all the different activities you've been learning and, even better, that you are beginning to make use of those opportunities. At this point, you may decide that it's time to retire your journal pages. But if you find them helpful or interesting, I would encourage you to continue to journal. For your last official journal assignment, take time this week to go back through your journal from the beginning of the book, all the way back to Week 1, and read your notes, noticing any changes that you have recorded.

What areas have changed for you? Which ones have stayed relatively similar? How do you feel about that? Write a summary of what you've learned, how you have changed, any goals you may have for the future, how you feel about this process, and whatever you need to complete this process.

Namaste.

CHAPTER 7

The Nature of the True Gift

As the word got out about me writing this book, an interesting thing began to happen. People approached me and began to tell me their stories. The impulse came not from wanting to give input on the book itself but perhaps more from a desire to convey their experience to someone who might have a greater understanding and sympathy for that experience. Or maybe it's just the natural human impulse to share stories, and since I was telling a story, they felt open to share theirs. Either way, I was more than happy to listen and to receive them. It was a blessing.

I want to share with you one of the last stories I received. Almost twenty years ago, "Dave" got a divorce under somewhat contentious circumstances and needed to have his wife and her young child leave his house. He found this "very unsettling":

How did I get into this mess? Where is my wisdom?
Where is my ground, my level being? I needed time, but
more than that, I needed to know what I was going to
learn from this crazy situation.

About a month into this, he was approached by a couple who hired him to do some work for a new meditation center they were starting. After getting acquainted, they came out to visit Dave, bringing several of their students to his house on the river. They took a pontoon boat out, and one of the teachers directed him to take them into a backwater.

I turned off the motor. No words of instruction, we all just
looked out, and finally heard the silence, the peaceful, gentle
feeling of floating on water. We stayed there two hours ... no
words, no egos, no stories, no thinking, just being.

The lesson I learned was not the letting go, but find-
ing a new stairway inside to a peaceful place. After some
months of trying on this new practice, I saw that me, the
outward, jovial, friendly person, and me, the inner quiet
person, were two different people. I like both sides of me,
but the quiet person was ... not needy, just about being.

During a Zen retreat at a rural retreat center, I sat, I
did not process, and I learned how to find myself again and
again. A light went on, and I discovered that earned silence

is better than filling up space with words. I no longer need to … create security to fill my insecurity, or to have attention focused on me. I do not need strokes or people to tell me I am okay. I know who I am and what I am not.

This ability to let go, of neediness, of striving and craving, and to let the silent voice of your own being have room to arrive—this is the gift. This is what really creates a place more immune to worry, anger, and anxiety. Becoming authentically yourself is incredibly powerful and profoundly calming. So don't give up. Keep exploring your opportunities to be more present with yourself and to find a quiet mind. That is where you really begin.

Going Forward

Which of the ways of quieting your mind and being more present you choose, when you choose to do them, and where you choose to practice them are going to vary. Some of the variables will have to do with circumstances, such as where you are (at work? in the car? at home?), whom you are with, what comes to mind first, which of the various things you've learned you like doing best … you get the idea.

But there are other things that can have an influence on you and your choices as well. After I had started meditating regularly, I began to play with it a little bit—sitting outside, looking out over a lake, eyes closed, eyes open, on a moving bus … you get the idea.

One summer was bracketed by two interesting experiences with sitting meditation. It began when I was at the Powderhorn Park MayDay Festival. This is a very cool, very big festival at the beginning of May that begins with the *best parade ever*, that winds its way to a large park where there is an enormous pageant, followed by stage performances, booths, food trucks, and entertainment of all kinds. Close to 50,000 people attend each year, so although it's not packed, it's alive with people, noise, and jubilant, post-winter good cheer.

Waiting for the festival to begin, I ended up sitting for a short while near people with whom I was having some complicated family dynamics and feeling a lot of complicated emotions. I decided this would be a great opportunity to meditate, especially since I was open to experimenting with my sitting.

The experience was profound. The hum and noise and activity of the crowd set up a vital cushion of energy that embraced and supported me. Rather than it becoming a distraction, it felt like the hum of the universe; I could feel the edges of myself, my ego, my identity, gently softening and joining the crowd, feathering into the larger pattern of people, planet, and beyond.

At the end of the same summer, I was at the Minnesota State Fair, waiting for my companions to get some food, and I decided to sit on the curb (finding those opportunities to sit wherever they may arise!) and quiet my mind. Again, a similar experience to May Day.

I tell you this not because I want to convince you that you should go into large crowds and practice mindfulness. I know that is not ideal for many or maybe even most people. And that's the point. I happen to be an extrovert. When I told my teacher about my experiences he said, "You must be an extrovert because being around other people calms and quiets your mind." If you've ever met me, the first part is pretty obvious, but I didn't know the second was an option.

I have plenty of introverted friends who find that sort of thing exhausting. Even at retreats, where everyone is focused inwardly and there is no speaking or interaction, they can find the proximity of so many people difficult for their practice, at least at first, while others feel really supported by sharing their practice with others.

Another condition that can influence your choice of how to approach being more present is your unique style of interacting with and processing information from the world. If you've ever taken a learning styles assessment or a Myers-Briggs test, you know that some of us lead from the gut, others from the head, and some are all about embodiment. Do you consider the world in visual terms? Is your go-to way of gathering information auditory or kinesthetic (via your body experience)? Your particular style will always be a combination of things, but a couple of them will be the most comfortable for you. As a result, you will probably find yourself tending toward using those techniques that fit into your comfort zone. Since the goal at this point is to find the path to being more present that you think of first, works best, comes easiest, and you feel most comfortable with, this is fine.

If you'd like to expand your horizons, I recommend that you take a look at the techniques and exercises you have spent less time with, and try them out when you have time and interest to do so.

Rewiring Your Brain

While you've been practicing the things you've been learning over the last six weeks, something crazy cool magical has been happening. You've been slowly rewiring your brain. Research has definitely shown that we can create new neural pathways in our brains, and experimenting with quieting your mind and exploring the self can help you make or strengthen connections in your brain that can make it work in new ways.

Researchers are finding that practicing being more mindful actually changes the structure of your brain, making connections between areas of the brain that were not well connected before and actually growing brain matter in some places. The increased brain matter has been seen to develop in the areas of the brain that deal with things like emotional regulation, attention, self-awareness, introspection, and compassion. There has even been shown regrowth in areas that have diminished in volume, showing that the damaging effects of some brain experiences are actually reversible with regular mindfulness practice. The one part of the brain that shows a *decrease* in gray matter is around the amygdala, a portion of the brain that has to do with fear and stress.

Getting in your daily walk or swim, or going to the gym, changes your body, decreasing fat, increasing circulation, increasing your flexibility, and making your tissues stronger. In the same way, regularly turning your attention to being mindful can make your brain function in a way that is stronger, healthier, and more relaxed and responsive.

The Mindful Athlete

One of the places I have seen interesting and powerful results from practicing mindfulness is in working with athletes. Focus is crucial in any type of physical activity in order to retain good form, maintain a clear visualization of outcome, and dispose of the kind of mental noise that can easily turn a win into a loss. Learning how to bring a mindful presence onto the court, field, or course can be the thing that takes your performance from good to very good, and from very good to great.

The issues of getting caught up in the past and in the future are as much in play while playing sports as anywhere else in your day—and depending on the perceived pressure of the situation, sometimes even more so, as in a high-pressure, competitive situations, for example. This is when many athletes get themselves "psyched out" or "too into their head." Suddenly you're fighting a case of the nerves and begin to suffer some performance anxiety.

Overthinking is one of the biggest stumbling blocks to a good performance, causing you to choke or fumble—this has been called "paralysis by analysis." What happens is the executive functions of the brain get overly involved and overwhelm the muscle memory and neural pathways that long practice and drills have made possible and were reinforced in your lower brain areas. Quieting that thinking part of the brain doesn't mean you should play nonstrategically or without any plan. It creates that spaciousness that allows the body to do its job, and lets opportunities and strategies open up and reveal themselves clearly—and with all the time and space in the world for you to act on them.

We have already talked about what happens in your body and mind when you are in a clutch situation and the adrenaline starts. You get some good, quick twitch muscle action going, but you start to lose parts of your vision, especially peripheral vision, the part that is best at picking up movement. Your mind starts to race, and your mind gets reactive instead of strategic.

Bringing your mind back to the present moment, and only the present moment, allows you to let go of that last bad serve, or that ill-considered decision, and prevents you from getting caught up in worrying about the things you fear will happen. By now, you've already begun to see some of the miraculous and ultimately helpful things that happen when you quiet your mind and turn your attention fully toward the present moment.

We've talked about the way time and space open up, even just a little bit, when you start to bring your mind to a place of quiet. Think about what you could do with that extra time when you are in the heat of competition. You could see the pitch as it approaches the plate. You could see another player lining up for a particular play or to execute a particular strategy. You could take that time for yourself to be sure that you are setting yourself up perfectly for your stroke, your shot, your pass, your spike.

And you can do all of these things without anxiety, worry, or nerves, because all that matters is what is happening right now in this moment. You are clear, relaxed, and responsive.

When you feel yourself beginning to get tight and anxious, or notice your heart and breath rates climbing excessively, taking a moment to practice a breathing technique is a great intervention to physiologically short-circuit that path toward a case of the nerves. Using your sense of touch is a great way to come right back to the present moment in the middle of the action—touch the ball, your racket, the edge of your sleeve. Feel the fabric of your clothing against your skin. Let yourself really take five or ten seconds to hear the sounds around you without attaching any meaning or importance to them.

Whether you are feeling wound up and spun out because your team is ahead or because you're worried about being behind in the score, getting back into the present moment will bring you into a state of clarity and equanimity that is invaluable when trying to make your body perform at its peak and your mind stay sharp and in the game.

Looking Forward
While Staying in the Moment

One thing that seems to confuse people who are learning about being present and mindful is the appropriate way to consider the future, to make plans, and even to daydream. It is important to me that you understand that I don't want you to think there is anything wrong with looking forward toward your future, planning, and dreaming. When I talk about the importance of being in the present and warn of the problems of thinking into the future, that can often cause people to wonder how both these things can be true—that you should be in the present and that it is not only good but necessary to be able to look into the future. There are a few things that will help you understand that this seemingly conflicting set of instructions is not actually in conflict at all.

First of all, the problem is not thinking about the future, it's about getting sucked into it. When you're thinking about the things that you need to do, want to do, or might do starts to disconnect from what, where, and how you are now, that's when the problems of worry and anxiety start to take hold. This is the phenomenon I referred to as "time travel" in an earlier part of the book.

When this begins to happen, it's not that you are planning or considering options or weighing possible outcomes; you've started to slip into a physical sense of actually being in that place in the future (or in the past) where you are suffering the effects of the events that you are concerned about happening. Events, let me remind you, that not only have not happened, but may not ever unfold in the way that you've anticipated or projected as happening. These events are entirely a fiction created by you out of time and space.

The difference is being conscious of your activity. Are you right here, right now, in this time and place, planning, considering, and dreaming? Or have you "left the building," disconnected from the present? You don't have to be dreamy or lost in thought for you to be slipping into future worry. You don't have to be firmly grounded in your sensory experience of the room, place, and physical characteristics of the place you are in in order to be present. Daydreaming can be a conscious choice. Sitting in a comfortable chair and letting your mind drift pleasantly along is something you can allow yourself to do mindfully.

The real question is, is the way you are allowing your mind to behave causing you distress? Are you checking out? Are you creating drama, anxiety, or unfounded anticipation? If any of these things are true, it's time to check back in using your favorite anchor or technique. You'll find your heart rate slows down and your body relaxes as you let go of the false sense of truth you've invested in the future.

The Creative Mind in the Present Moment

One of the things I see happening a lot with the creation of a more spacious mind is that the opportunities for creative thoughts to arise increase dramatically. Although there have been studies done on the connection between mindfulness and creativity, and there seems to be a universal agreement that there is one, no one really knows why learning to be mindful brings a creative spark to our lives.

Not only can learning to quiet the mind and be present instill creativity, it also has the ability to open up creative blocks. Think about the anxiety and noisy chattering of the mind that can arise as you get more and more tied up in trying to resolve a problem or find yourself blind to options and possibilities.

As your mind becomes more spacious and the chatter begins to fade into the background, the mind begins to have a better sense of the big picture, able to "see the forest for the trees." The mind steps away from the specific details and niggling little problems and gets a sort of bird's-eye view of your ideas and your projects. This overview brings new perspective and gets the little stuff out of the way.

Creative thinking and problem solving are boosted by this quieter mind whether the spark of creativity is needed to create a sculpture, a piece of music, or a new way to design a circuit board or solve a troubling astrophysics problem.

One artist friend sees mindfulness practice as being inseparably linked with her creative process. She finds that the ways that quieting her mind assists her creative processes are broad and numerous. "Art is about seeing things that other people miss," she says. Being mindful gives her the insight to find those things and give them voice:

> *Being able to create while being in the present moment*
> *has the effect of putting a damper on the critical voice,*
> *keeping it from cutting off creativity. Editing is where*
> *the rational mind comes in, but that comes later.*

Letting go of the ego, the judging mind, coming back to the present moment so that you can respond to what is there, in front of you, rather than trying to apply a formula lets creativity have its own way.

The problem I experience is that when I am meditating and I have creative ideas or great solutions to problems pop into my head, what do I do with them? Some people keep a notebook handy where they can jot a quick one- or two-word note to remind themselves, but one artist said, "I just trust that the good ideas have staying power, and that I'll have no trouble recalling them later."

Developing a regular practice of being present and mindful has the power to change your life from the office to the golf course to wherever you find your creative voice. It is a lifelong gift you give yourself, and of course, to others around you.

Namaste.

CHAPTER 8

The Mindfulness Habit and Special Issues

As more awareness is arising around mindfulness and its ability to actually change our brain physiology, there is a growing acceptance of the fact that it has the ability to do more than just mellow you out when you're having a bad day.

Attention-based mindfulness techniques are being explored by researchers and medical professionals as a support for resolving a wide variety of behavioral and health issues. In the years that I've been practicing and teaching mindfulness, I have been exposed to a number of these, and I have to say, I continue to be taken aback at how effective and powerful using the mind's own ability to quiet itself can be at resolving issues that for years were only thought to be addressable by medication or other, less self-led approaches. Depending on the severity of these issues, who you are, and how much other support you have, you may find that employing the things you've learned in the last several weeks can be a powerful addition to the approaches you are already taking to work with the challenges you face.

Sometimes people have even found that learning how to be more present and mindful can not only supplement their coping strategies but can actually replace them. *If you are interested in doing this, please do so under the guidance of a professional in the field who understands your needs.*

Attention Issues and the Quieted Mind

I was close to forty years old when my mentor and friend turned to me and said, "You know you're ADD, right?" Because I have a lot of respect for him, and I know he doesn't carry a lot of judgment about this sort of thing, and because he identifies with having a mind that functions this way as well, I was open to his comment, and I let it sit and ferment for a while.

I believe that deep down I knew he was on the money, and yet I could not see any problems in the way my brain works. In fact, I think it's kind of cool. I am constantly fascinated by the way it takes two superficially unrelated, disconnected things and finds out where they connect and how they enhance each other, coming together to create something entirely new. He and I talked about this, and we agreed that our experience was very similar. I like to think of ADD as "Attention Distribution Difference." I feel like I have a lot of attention, but it seems like it is important to my mind to distribute it in a lot of different directions at different times.

I tell you this because although I embrace the workings of my amazing brain and the way it draws together wildly disparate sources of information and ideas to make unusual and unique connections, it has also served as a source of frustration at various times in my life. But I find that I don't really struggle with the downsides to this way of thinking anymore. I've been lucky enough to be given the opportunity to develop my mind in a way that gives me the power to quiet and focus it by practicing mindfulness.

One day I took an assessment for ADD, but I took it twice. The first time I took it as if it were a dozen or so years earlier, back before I started pursuing a meditation practice. I thought about who I was at the time and how I functioned, and then I dug down deep and thought about how I would have answered the questions. I will tell you I was actually surprised at how solidly I came up well within the spectrum of ADD. Then I took it again as the person I am now, with the way that I now function, and my score indicated that I was comfortably outside the range for that diagnosis.

The thing is, as much as I value the unique properties of the way my mind connects the unusual and disparate, I also value the ability to quiet some of that chatter when I want to. By becoming a regular meditator, I managed to keep the really cool things about the way my mind functions, but I now remain more firmly in the driver's seat. I am more patient, present, and, frankly, happy.

It may seem odd to some people that the appropriate solution to not being able to pay attention is to pay more attention, but it's not that strange if you think of it like this. If I have a weak muscle, I can either adjust all my activities to accommodate that and work around it, letting it atrophy and grow so weak that it becomes useless, or I can work to strengthen the muscle so that I can function in an easier, more balanced way.

Developing the Mindfulness Habit is like strengthening that muscle. It not only creates the neural pathways that allow the mind to automatically want to be more present, but it allows you to be able to see and recognize when the mind is starting to rev up before it begins to spin out of control. So the mindfulness becomes not only a remedy but also a preventative.

Having a habit for being more mindful that extends throughout the activities of the day becomes particularly important for this population of people, probably more than anyone else. Those of us with unusual attention distribution can find ourselves spinning off on anything at any time, so having this skill of being able to become fully present easily and immediately can save a lot of frustration for ourselves and others and improve quality of life.

I can comfortably say that my brain still makes connections between strange and wonderful things in ways that create something new and beautiful, only now I can pay attention to them long enough to remember them.

Some people with an ADD diagnosis have a lot of trouble focusing and staying with a task, some fidget and have trouble keeping their body still, including their tendency to talk excessively, and others show impatience, tend to interrupt others, and have trouble interacting appropriately. Most have a combination of these things, weighted in a particular direction.

In each of these cases, learning how to come into the present moment, quiet the mind, and be able to find that sense of spaciousness can be powerful in shifting the ability to slow down, be more present, and make life easier to handle in ways that are socially appropriate. Stillness, patience, and focus are all clear outcomes of a regular mindfulness practice, and especially one that is geared toward everyday functioning.

The level of commitment and the length of time that it might take for someone whose brain functions in this way may be a bit more, but the payoff is very great. The changes in staying present really show up starkly when you have a brain that tends to wander far and wide.

Mental Health and Being in the Present Moment

I want to start off by saying that I am not a mental health professional and that I have great sympathy for those who struggle with issues around their mental health. I am also impressed with those people who have, through working with mindfulness or combining it with well-regulated medication, found a way to lead a healthy life.

There has been a lot of work in the mental health community with using mindfulness-related therapies for treating a variety of issues. Dialectical behavior therapy (DBT), for example, begins with a mindfulness approach, developing the skill of being in the present moment. This allows the participant to experience their circumstances and how they are responding in a way that allows for developing a more nonjudgmental approach and greater equanimity around them.

One person's story about good mental health and mindfulness is that it became obvious when she was in her early twenties that she needed to start medication for severe depression and social anxiety disorder. The medication produced its own set of issues that were then addressed by an additional diagnosis, which was also treated with medication. By the time she had reached the peak of being medicated, she was taking thirty-three pills a day! She decided to wean herself off of medication by renewing her commitment to regular meditation, throwing herself into daily practice in order "to just be."

Although she felt better, she still had a level of anxiety that caused her to feel the need to run or hide, and moving into work and life was a struggle every day. She went back on a single, more carefully chosen medication, which worked in balance with her mindfulness practice to take it deeper. "Mindfulness practice literally saved my life," she says. "I need to have both (medication and meditation) in order to be there for other people, to be someone who is not erratic and can exist in a moment and have equanimity. I am eternally grateful for the practice."

When it comes to depression, there is definitely a spectrum, and those who find themselves so deep in it that they are unable to function are first on the list of those who should seek medical care, especially if they are having thoughts about harming themselves or others.

There is a growing number of medical professionals who are now being more circumspect about the use of SSRIs and other medication traditionally prescribed for depression, feeling that the increased information about the side effects of medication, along with new questions about their efficacy, may weigh against their use in cases of mild or moderate depression.

So what alternatives to medication are being proposed by these professionals? Mindfulness and meditation are at the top of the list. The aspects of depression that being mindful has been shown to counteract are numerous. But most important among them are the tendency to brood and get caught in a self-perpetuating spiral of depressive feelings, and the problems that come with fragmented attention, something which has been shown to be detrimental to our mental and emotional health in general.

Feelings of depression "hijack" your attention. They are very self-perpetuating and can easily create a cycle that drags you further and further down into that sense of hopelessness. Finding a way to bring yourself back into the simplicity of the present moment can put the brakes on this spiral and shift the attention back out to the anchor. Some people have described it as letting some fresh air into their mind.

In my experience, using one of the senses as an anchor is a really effective way to shift your focus in these circumstances. It has the advantages of being physical, drawing the attention outside the mind, and is often gratifyingly pleasant. The pleasantness of the experience is a nice break from the looming darkness that comes as depression spirals in, and gives a lovely respite for the mind, even if only for a moment.

There is no question that the things you have learned here are ideal for addressing issues around fragmented attention. As you have certainly found by now, just making the decision to stop and pay attention to one thing for a few moments changes how you feel about multitasking, distraction, and the importance of the present moment.

If you are like me, the simple pleasures of life that are revealed when you allow yourself to completely enter the present moment are a powerful antidote to feelings of depression. For me, the pleasures of being alive, in a body, on this planet, all come into sharp focus when I am completely and totally here, at least for a moment. The Buddha called it "this precious human life."

Obsessive compulsive disorder of various kinds also responds well to mindfulness. In fact, one person I spoke with was being primarily treated for this through dialectical behavior therapy. DBT is directly derived from Buddhist meditation practices and has been useful for emotion regulation and mood disorders.

I am not in any way recommending that you dump your prescribed drug routine, but I have had clients—*under a doctor's supervision*—integrate these techniques into a weaning off of or diminishment in dosage of their medication. The decision is a personal one, and should be considered carefully and responsibly.

Even if you don't choose to change your medication routine, understand that what you've learned here is a very valuable aid for gaining the upper hand on chronic depression and other issues of mental health. Adding mindfulness to your self-care routine is something to consider embracing as a great adjunct to other ways of taking care of yourself.

Addiction and Mindfulness

As with the previous topic, with this subject we wander into some very tricky territory. I do not have any kind of special training in working with addiction issues (although I have shared this information and worked with people who have history of addiction), but I wanted to make sure you knew that out in the recovery community, mindfulness practices are being more and more embraced as a great support for those who are in recovery, both in the early stages and in maintenance.

When one of my friends was young, he suffered from undiagnosed issues around bipolar disorder that led him to start self-medicating with alcohol. He was so unaware that his behavior was outside the healthy norm that he was drinking a case of beer a night and thinking it was a reasonable amount. After being medicated for his mental health issues, he decided to stop drinking, but his efforts only lasted three days. He realized after a few weeks that he was going to need help.

In college, he had been part of a meditation community, but a variety of circumstances had led him to walk away from it for a while. After going through recovery, "church shopping" ended up leading him back to meditation and to a community. He says, "Mindfulness reminds me that I am part of something larger." He believes that this is an important antidote to what he sees as the selfishness of addiction.

Another member of the recovery community told me that he found that going to AA meetings was about being wholeheartedly present to others as they shared their experience. When he found his way into mindfulness practice, he thought, "This is the same thing, only another person's not talking. Of course, it turns out I was talking—all the time." He feels mindfulness helps him be present to others' suffering; not running away from it, just being with it.

He affirms that addiction is essentially self-centered and that being open and present works counter to that.

Many meditation and Buddhist centers now open their doors to twelve-step communities or have their own recovery programs. In these places, recovery is very much supported by meditation, mindfulness, and other adjunct, complementary practices. In fact, the eleventh step includes "meditation and prayer," building the possibility of mindfulness practice right into the program.

The ability to come into the present moment and remain there is a powerful tool in the fight against addiction. Shifting your awareness to the idea that there is this moment, and only this moment, that the past is gone, the future does not exist, and that by the time you recognize that, this fleeting moment is gone as well, can help you survive any number of unpleasant sensations, cravings, fears, and discomfort.

When my sister quit smoking, she learned a lot about addiction. The first thing she learned was that nicotine cravings lasted three minutes. Knowing that she only needed to deal with those feelings for three minutes made it possible for her to ride them out. Knowing you only need to deal with the kind of forces that drive addicts toward relapse for the length of each moment as it arrives makes it possible to get through some of the tougher stretches. Each one of these events or sensations is a temporary state of affairs; they have no permanence.

The diminished stress that comes from learning to be more present certainly is an additional level of support for dealing with addiction. This approach to making moments of stress opportunities for being present—turning them on their head and making them work for you as a positive habit—makes a great weapon in the fight against addiction. It is true that stress, trauma, and adversity are large motivators for slipping out of recovery, so anything you can do to reduce these feelings supports your recovery.

Trauma and Being Present in the Body

Not too long ago, I traveled out of state for an event that turned into a Jerry Springer–style freak show. I was hours from the nearest airport, trapped in a house of crazy, no car, and days away from my flight home. I ended up being rescued by some people whose own meltdown drama required me being rescued a second time.

By the time I got home, I was a mess. And I knew that I needed to get really present. I did a lot of mindfulness practice, including some things that were quite physical. I did them in a way that was concentrated and connected and mindful. The result was that week I cried in yoga, I cried in tai ji, and I cried at the morning chanting of Indian, Chinese, and Japanese names at my meditation center. I could see how broken the connection between my eyes, my mind, and my mouth was, and how I had disconnected from my body. Within ten days I was no longer finding myself mysteriously in tears, having nightmares, or having unpleasant and uncomfortable digestive issues.

Trauma can get really stuck in our bodies as well as our minds. Being able to become mindful is a very powerful way to reconnect with your mind and body, connecting them to the present moment and to each other.

Normal trauma moves into a state called posttraumatic stress disorder (PTSD) when the normal response to trauma gets stuck. After a trauma, the mind and body are in shock, but then you process your feelings and experiences and the shock goes away. PTSD happens when you remain in a state of shock, as your memories and how you feel about the event are disconnected. Facing feelings and memories is important to stop the stuck and resolve it.

Posttraumatic stress disorder is a complicated set of symptoms that can result from a variety of extreme traumatic events, including war, assault, injury, or disaster. What those events were, the individual character and experience of the person who was subjected to them, as well as cultural and family history factors all play a role in how these issues are expressed.

Studies by the U.S. Department of Veterans Affairs ("Potential of Mindfulness in Treating Trauma Reactions") have shown, however, that bringing mindfulness into treatment has a widely positive effect for PTSD sufferers, either as an ancillary or primary treatment.

A former longtime member of the Tripler Army Medical Center's psychiatric team says about his extensive experience working with PTSD that one of the basic necessities of the body is to know where it is. Trauma stress injury (as he prefers to call it) affects the ability of the body to recognize where it is. He has seen mindfulness, especially in relationship to the body, to be an effective way of bringing that recognition back. The result is a diminishment of many of the symptoms such as hyper-vigilance and alienation.

From assisting with chronic pain, to dispersing the effects of hyper-arousal, to laying important groundwork for other therapeutic techniques, the ability to bring oneself fully into the present moment has a profound effect on offsetting the difficulties that occur with PTSD.

Conclusion

My greatest hope for you as you move forward with this practice is that your developing ability to be more mindful and in the present moment will allow you to be part of the world in a more peaceful way. And I will go out on a limb and promise you that if you continue in your practice to let yourself live more mindfully in the present moment, the returns on that investment will be numerous and unexpected.

Don't be surprised to see yourself become increasingly patient and tolerant, to being less easily rattled by the unexpected, to be a source of stability and comfort for others. But for now, just practice for your own sake, and for the sake of this particular moment and all it has to offer. Don't go looking for anything else. Don't worry, the gifts will find you.

As you've spent the last month and a half (or maybe longer) experimenting with some different ways of bringing yourself more fully into the present moment, you most certainly have noticed something has changed. The changes may be subtle or obvious; they may have come upon you gradually, or with a big "aha!"

Change is good—it's what you were looking for, after all—but change can be hard. As you begin to find a more quiet mind, and a more relaxed and present way of living your life day to day, you may notice that some of the things you took for granted as part of your everyday life, things you didn't mind, or things you even liked, no longer seem to fit. It can be a very disconcerting feeling.

If you find yourself in this place where you feel like you are experiencing some kind of friction in your interactions with situations, people, or events where things just don't feel right, use the skills you've been learning. Stop, breathe, quiet your mind. Let your attention rest on your senses and on your sense of your body. When you rest in that place of quiet, it will allow you to see things with greater equanimity and spaciousness. From this place you can get a clearer view of the situation, let some of the baggage slip away, and reexamine your relationship to your circumstances.

Whatever you do, don't throw the baby out with the bathwater. Change can be difficult enough that you may find it tempting to negate the things that have brought it about, but remember all the ways that you're finding benefit from what you been practicing and keep working on staying in the present moment.

You are now on your way to becoming one of those people—the ones who can be depended on to stay solid in an emergency, to not foster drama, to keep your head about you when all others are losing theirs. A gift to not only yourself but to others. And we all thank you.

Namaste.

Bibliography

Charles Duhigg, *The Power of Habit: Why We Do What We Do in Life and Business* (New York: Random House, 2012).

Britta K. Hölzela, James Carmodyc, Mark Vangela, Christina Congletona, Sita M. Yerramsettia, Tim Garda, and Sara W. Lazar, "Mindfulness Practice Leads to Increases in Regional Brain Gray Matter Density," http://www. umassmed.edu/uploadedFiles/cfm2/Psychiatry_Resarch _Mindfulness.pdf.

Jon Kabat-Zinn, *Wherever You Go, There You Are: Mindfulness Meditation in Everyday Life* (New York: Hyperion, 2005).

——*Full Catastrophe Living: Using the Wisdom of Your Body and Mind to Face Stress, Pain, and Illness* (New York: Bantam Books, 2013).

Vujanovic, Niles, Pietrefesa, Potter, and Schmertz, U.S.
Department of Veterans Affairs, National Center for
PTSD, http://www.ptsd.va.gov/professional/treatment
/overview/mindful-PTSD.asp.

To Write to the Author

If you wish to contact the author or would like more information about this book, please write to the author in care of Llewellyn Worldwide Ltd. and we will forward your request. Both the author and publisher appreciate hearing from you and learning of your enjoyment of this book and how it has helped you. Llewellyn Worldwide Ltd. cannot guarantee that every letter written to the author can be answered, but all will be forwarded. Please write to:

Kate Sciandra
℅ Llewellyn Worldwide
2143 Woodale Drive
Woodbury, MN 55125-2989

Please enclose a self-addressed stamped envelope for reply, or $1.00 to cover costs. If outside the U.S.A., enclose an international postal reply coupon.

Many of Llewellyn's authors have websites with additional information and resources. For more information, please visit our website at http://www.llewellyn.com.